The Legal Writing Handbook

Practice Book
Second Edition
✦✦✦

Laurel Currie Oates
Anne Enquist
Kelly Kunsch

all of Seattle University School of Law

Aspen Law & Business
A Division of Aspen Publishers, Inc.

ISBN   1-56706-938-X

This publication is designed to provide accurate and authoritative information in regard to the subject matter covered. It is sold with the understanding that the publisher is not engaged in rendering legal, accounting, or other professional services. If legal advice or other professional assistance is required, the services of a competent professional person should be sought.

> -- From a <u>Declaration of Principles</u> jointly adopted by a Committee of the American Bar Association and Committee of Publishers and Associations.

1 2 3 4 5

Table of Contents

✦PART II: WRITING

Introduction

The adage "practice makes perfect" is true for many things, including writing and legal research. This text is designed as a supplement to *The Legal Writing Handbook* so that students can practice the writing and research skills that they learned in the *Handbook*.

Notice that the second half of *The Practice Book for the Legal Writing Handbook* is the "Answer Key" for the writing exercises. In the Answer Key, you will often find short explanations about why a given answer is recommended.

In these explanations, the Answer Key often refers to specific rules in the *Handbook* and uses specific grammatical terms. The rules and grammar terminology are included to help students better understand why suggested answers are correct or effective or both. They are not the answers themselves. Consequently, students using the book should not feel that they have to cite a specific rule or use a technical grammar term in order to answer an exercise question correctly.

To determine when a given exercise is applicable, see the references in the *Handbook*.

Research
Exercises
✦✦✦

Chapter 11
Constitutions and Charters

✦EXERCISE 11.A - USE OF CONSTITUTIONS

1.   What part of the federal constitution concerns unreasonable searches or seizures?

2.   List two U.S. Supreme Court cases decided within the last year discussing what constitutes an illegal search.

✦For the following questions, look in the constitution of one of the following states: South Carolina, Maine, Idaho, Michigan, or Arkansas.

3.   What jurisdiction are you researching in?

4.   What part of the state constitution concerns unreasonable searches or seizures?

5.   Is the language used in the state constitution exactly the same as that used in the U.S. Constitution?

6.   Give a cite to a law review article discussing the above state constitutional provision.

Chapter 12
The Legislative Branch

✦**EXERCISE 12.A - USE OF CODES**

1. Brenda and Eddie come to your office. They want to get married but their parents do not approve. Eddie is 16; Brenda is 14. For each question, give the answer and, where appropriate, the relevant citation for your authority.

✦Research this question in either: New York, Florida, Arizona, Missouri, or West Virginia

  a. What jurisdiction are you researching in?

  b. Can Brenda and Eddie get married without their parents permission?

  c. At what age can/could they marry?

  d. Does it matter if Brenda is pregnant?

  e. If Brenda and Eddie are second cousins (they have the same great-grandmother), can they get married?

2. You work at the prosecutor's office. A suspect has been apprehended and it is your job to charge him with the appropriate crime. The alleged facts are that he came up behind a middle-aged woman, held a knife to her throat and demanded her wallet. The woman handed over her wallet which contained $20 cash and credit cards. The suspect allegedly

took the wallet and ran off. Give the answer to each question and, where appropriate, the citation to the governing authority.

✦Research this question in either: Pennsylvania, Oregon, Georgia, Oklahoma, or North Dakota.

    a.   What jurisdiction are you researching in?

    b.   What crime would you charge the suspect with?

    c.   What class of crime is the charge (*e.g.*, felony, misdemeanor, etc.)?

    d.   What is the maximum sentence or sentencing range if the suspect is convicted of the crime (if necessary, assume this is his first offense)?

    e.   When was this sentencing statute first enacted? How many times has it been amended?

3.   In what year was the Jones-Connally Farm-Relief Act passed? (hints: it is a federal act and you should use the popular names table.)

4.   Where is the FDIC Assessment Rate Act of 1990 codified?

5.   One of the basic documents of Indian law is referred to as "Public Law 280." Although rarely mentioned, it was passed by the 83d Congress (67 Stat. 588). Based on this information, tell where it is currently codified in the U.S.C..

6.   Using an annotated code, give citations to two cases discussing "fair use" of copyrighted works (hint: copyright is a federal issue).

✦EXERCISE 12.B - LEGISLATIVE HISTORY

✦You have been assigned to uncover some information about the National Endowment for the Arts. More specifically, your employer wants to know some of the criticisms that were made about the agency at the time of its creation.

1.   Using the index, find where in the United States Code enacting legislation for the Endowment is. Give the citation.

2.   At the end of the statutory text, you will find the dates of enactment and amendment for the act. What is the date that the act was first passed?

3.   What is the date of the most recent amendment (remember pocket parts and other supplements)?

4.   Focusing on the original enactment, what is the public law number?

5.   Find *Sources of Compiled Legislative Histories* (by Nancy P. Johnson) in your library. Is there previously compiled legislative history for the act?

6.   Find the act in the *United States Code Congressional and Administrative News* (USCCAN) volumes (the acts are arranged by public law number). What is the cite in USCCAN for the text of the bill as it first passed?

Note: The text as it appears in the above is the same as that in the Statutes at Large. On occasion, if you need to research the law in a bygone year, you may be forced to rely on these to piece together the text.

7.   What page does the Laws portion of USCCAN refer you to for legislative history?

8.   Go to the page you were referred to above. What days was the bill considered in Congress (realize that you could go to the *Congressional Record* for those days to find records of floor debates)?

9.   Peruse the House Report reprinted in USCCAN. Give two reasons why the minority viewpoint recommended that the bill be rejected.

◆For legislative history after 1970, the CIS service is more comprehensive than USCCAN. Locate the CIS service in you library. The legislation on the National Endowment of the Arts was amended in 1985 by P.L. 99-194. Locate this legislation in the CIS Legislative Histories volume for 1985.

10.   How many Congressional Reports are available?

◆Notice that the reports and hearings are available in full text in microfiche published by CIS. Cites to the dates of consideration (for accessing the *Congressional Record*) and other documents and miscellaneous publications are also mentioned if relevent.

◆You should also be aware that for recent legislation, LEXIS and WESTLAW have a variety of legislative history sources available. The *Congressional Record* is available on both systems. Bills, Reports, and other documents pertaining to Congressional legislation may also be available.

11.   *(optional)* Using either LEXIS or WESTLAW, find recent criticisms of the National Endowment of the Arts made by members of Congress in the *Congressional Record*. Give the cite to one of these statements.

Chapter 13
The Executive Branch and Administrative Agencies

✦EXERCISE 13.A - ADMINISTRATIVE REGULATIONS

Federal Register

Remember that in order for administrative regulations to be valid, the governing agency must comply with certain procedures in promulgating them. Notice of proposed rulemaking and a period for comment are part of these procedures. The notice and information concerning how and when comments can be made are published in the *Federal Register*.

✦Locate a recent copy of the *Federal Register*.

1.   What is the date of the issue you are using?

✦Look in the Contents section at the beginning of the issue. Find a heading for proposed rules under one of the agencies. Go to that page.

2.   What agency is proposing the rule?

3.   What section of the Code of Federal Regulations will the proposed rule affect?

4.   What date must comments be received by?

✦Now locate the volume of the Code of Regulations which the proposed rule would affect. Look at the cover of the volume.

5.   When was the CFR volume you are using last revised?

◆Find the section that your proposed rule would affect.

6.   What is the heading for your section?

7.   What is the authority for the section? (this means what section of the United States Code grants the agency the authority to promulgate regulations governing the area of law. The authority is usually listed at the beginning of each part or subpart. A regulation can be challenged if it is without authority or if it exceeds the granted authority.)

◆Normally, if you want to find regulations on a subject, you start with the code itself, specifically, with the index. Using the index to the CFR, find the regulation governing bicycle safety.

8.   What is the cite to the relevant section?

9.   What agency promulgated these regulations?

◆Notice the "SOURCE" notation at the beginning of the section. It tells you when the section was enacted and where in the *Federal Register* such regulations were published unless otherwise noted.

10.   What subsection covers requirements for the seat?

11.   When was it amended?

◆Using the List of Sections Affected (LSA) volumes of the CFR, see if the above section has been amended since the last revision of the CFR (remember the date of the revision may vary from volume to volume of the CFR. The revision date appears on the cover of each volume).

12. Has any part of the section been amended? If so, what is the *Federal Register* cite to the amendment?

♦To further update, go to the most recent edition of the *Federal Register*. In the back is a table called "CFR parts affected during [month]." For whatever months are not covered by the List of Sections Affected, see if the above section has been amended.

13. Has any part of the section been amended after the most recent LSA? If so, what is the *Federal Register* cite to the amendment?

14. What is the name of the codification of your state's administrative regulations?

15. In your state codification, give the citation to the section(s) governing the state police or state patrol.

16. What published volumes, if any, update your state administrative code?

Chapter 14
The Judicial Branch

✦**EXERCISE 14.A - USE OF DIGESTS**

The community newspaper runs a critical article about a local law enforcement officer. Among other comments, the article says: "Sheriff John Brown has long been associated with members of organized crime. In fact, it is generally acknowledged that contributions received from such associates financed his successful campaign for sheriff." Brown wants to bring an action against the newspaper for defamation.

✦Use the Federal Digest to research these issues. Begin by using the Descriptive Word Index. If you are unable to find the specific key number using the index, browse the topic analysis for the appropriate topic to find the correct key number and answers to the questions.

1.   Under what West topic can most of the law of defamation be found?

2.   What are the elements for defamation generally?

3.   What key number did you find the above answer under?

4.   A major area of contention will be whether Sheriff John Brown is a public figure. Under what key number are cases discussing this issue?

5.   List two Court of Appeals cases discussing the public figure issue.

✦Remember that West key numbers are the same regardless of which digest you use. Therefore you will not need to use the Descriptive Word Index to find cases on the above topics in a different jurisdiction.

6.   Using the West digest for your home state, list two state cases discussing the defamation public figure issue.

7.   Using West's United States Supreme Court Digest (Table of Cases volume), give the citation to *Miranda v. Arizona*.

8.   How many times has the group Jews for Jesus been a party to a suit at the United States Supreme Court (hint: the answer can be found in the Defendant-Plaintiff Table volume)? Give the citation(s).

9.   Give the citation (pinpoint cite) to at least three federal cases decided after 1975 defining the phrase "latent defect."

Chapter 15
Secondary Sources

♦**EXERCISE 15.A - ENCYCLOPEDIAS**

Select one of the following legal issues:

> ♦false advertising or misrepresentation (generally)
>
> ♦physician's liability for acts of employees
>
> ♦right to inspect or search a prison inmate's mail
>
> ♦government licensing of thoroughbred horse racing
>
> ♦light shining on another's property as nuisance

♦Consult the index to Corpus Juris Secundum (C.J.S.). Locate an entry for your subject in it.

1.   What topic did you select?

2.   What terms did you look up in the index?

♦CJS is published by West. Notice, however, that the title and section are not related to the topic and key number in a West digest. If there is a reference to a West key number, it will be in a notation labeled "Library References."

3.   What title(s) and section number(s) does the index entry refer you to (list no more than two)?

♦Go to the bound volume that contains the title and section to one of your references. Before turning to the exact section you found in the index, look at the analysis (outline) of the title at the beginning of the title. After you have perused it to see what the title covers, turn to the section you found in question three.

4.   What is the name of the section?

5.   Give a citation to a case from a footnote that you might check if you wanted to find some primary authority on the issue.

6.   Are there any references to practice aids or other research tools listed in the section (remember to check the pocket part as well as the bound volume)?

◆Now go to the index volumes of American Jurisprudence, 2d Series (Am. Jur. 2d). Locate an entry for your subject in it.

7.   What terms did you look up in *this* index?

8.   What topic(s) and section number(s) does the index entry refer you to (again, list no more than two)?

◆After looking at the outline in the front of the topic, go to one of the sections that you found in question 8.

9.   What is the title of the section?

10.   Give the citation to a case from a footnote in Am. Jur. 2d that you might check if you wanted to find some primary authority on the issue.

11.   Are there any references to practice aids or other research tools listed in the section? If there are, give the citation to one of them.

Consult the Index to Annotations volume. Locate an ALR annotation on "who is a public figure."

1.   Give the citation to an annotation you found.

2.   Look in the to see if the annotation has been superseded. Has it? If so, give the citation to the superseding annotation and use it for the following questions.

3.   What exemplary case on the topic is fully reported in the volume?

4.   Is there a case from Hawaii cited by this particular annotation? If so, in what section of the annotation does it appear? What is its citation?

5.   Give the cite to a Pennsylvania case talking about the subject matter of §38[b]: doctor held not to be public figure (remember to consult pocket parts)

✦*Optional*: A.L.R. annotations are also searchable full-text on LEXIS, WESTLAW and CD-ROM. Using one of those services, find an annotation on the liability of a garage for damages to an automobile left on its premises for repair work.

6.   Using the Index to Annotations volume again, find an annotation about the right of a prevailing party to attorneys' fees under the Education of the Handicapped Act. Give the citation.

7.   Is the annotation still good? If not, give the citation to the superseding annotation.

8.   Give the citation to an annotation discussing the Uniform Simultaneous Death Act.

9.   Give the citation to an annotation discussing §58-37-13 of the Utah code.

✦*Optional*: ALR annotations are also searchable full-text on LEXIS and WESTLAW. Using one of those services, find an annotation on the liability of a garage for damages to a car or automobile left on its premises for repair work.

10.   What search(es) did you use?

11.   Give the citation to an annotation you located.

✦EXERCISE 15.C - TREATISES

Select one of the following treatises:

> ✦*The Law of Municipal Corporations* by Eugene McQuillin
> ✦*Page on the Law of Wills* by William Herbert Page
> ✦*The Law of Real Property* by Richard Roy Belden Powell
> ✦*Federal Practice and Procedure* by Charles Alan Wright and Arthur Raphael Miller
> ✦*Fletcher Cyclopedia of the Law of Private Corporations* by William Meade Fletcher
> ✦*Corbin on Contracts; a Comprehensive Treatise on the Rules of Contract Law* by Arthur Linton Corbin

✦Using your law library's catalog, locate an entry for the treatise you chose.

1.   Where in your library is the book located (include the book's call number as well as any other necessary information)?

✦Find the treatise in your library. Consult the index. Find a section discussing the following subject for your topic:

> ✦McQuillin - City's duty to clean sidewalks
> ✦Page - Definition of codicil
> ✦Powell - Remedies for nuisance
> ✦Wright & Miller - Forum non conveniens, generally

◆Fletcher - Effect of conflict of interest on quorum requirements
◆Corbin - Acceptance of offer by mail

2.   What terms did you find in the index that led you to the correct section(s).

3.   Give the correct bluebook citation to the section you located (remember to include the volume number as well as the section).

4.   List a case that is cited in the footnotes to the section that you just found.

◆Now use your library's catalog to find another book on the same general topic as the treatise you used.

5.   Give the author, title, and date of the book.

6.   What subject headings did you use to find the book?

◆EXERCISE 15.D - LAW REVIEWS

Select one of the following subjects:

◆Law of Native Americans (Indians)
◆Law of Corporate Takeovers
◆Law of Surrogate Parenting
◆Law of Drunken Driving
◆Law of Wrongful Dismissal from Employment

1.   Which subject did you choose?

2.   Looking in a volume of the *Index to Legal Periodicals* (ILP), what subject heading do you find articles about your subject under?

3.   Give the bluebook citation to one article under this heading.

4.   Now, looking in a volume of the *Current Law Index* (CLI), find a different article on your subject. What subject heading did you find the article under in CLI?

5.   Give the bluebook citation to one article under this heading.

Choose one of the following cases:

   ✦*National Collegiate Athletic Association v. Tarkanian*, 109 S. Ct. 454 (1988).
   ✦*City of Clearwater v. Studebaker's Dance Club*, 516 So. 2d 1106 (Fla. Dist. Ct. App. 1987).
   ✦*Falwell v. Flynt,* 797 F.2d 1270 (4th Cir. 1986).
   ✦*Polaroid Corp. v. Disney*, 862 F.2d 987 (3d Cir. 1988).
   ✦*In re Baby M.*, 537 A.2d 1227 (N.J. 1988).

✦Using the Table of Cases portion of either ILP or CLI, find an article about your case. Realize that articles about particular cases are most likely to be written shortly after the publication of the case.

6.   Which case did you select?

7.   Give the bluebook citation to an article about your case.

Choose one of the following authors:

   ✦Lawrence M. Friedman
   ✦Yale Kamisar
   ✦Janet E. Ainsworth
   ✦Richard A. Posner
   ✦Charles Alan Wright

8.   Give the bluebook citation to an article by your author.

✦Go to where the law reviews are shelved in your law library and look up the citation you found in either question two or question four.

9.   What type of work is it (e.g., article (by a nonstudent), student comment, casenote)?

10.   How many footnotes to the text are there?

✦EXERCISE 15.E AND 15.F - DICTIONARIES AND WORDS & PHRASES

Using a law dictionary, look up the definition (as it relates to the Sheriff John Brown case described in the Chapter 14 Exercise for digests) for one of the following:

> ✦publication
> ✦actual malice
> ✦defamation
> ✦libel
> ✦slander

1.   What dictionary did you use?

2.   Give the appropriate definition of the word or phrase.

3.   Is there a citation for authority for the definition? If so, give the citation.

✦Look the same term up in the multivolume *Words & Phrases* set.

4.   Give the citation to a case that defines the term.

✦Now, go to the *Words & Phrases* volume of your state or regional digest.

5. Give the citation to the most recent case in your state (if none, from your region) that defines the term.

6. Is the actual definition printed out in the digest volumes? Was it in the *Words & Phrases* set?

Chapter 16
Shepard's Citators

-

◆**EXERCISE 16.A -** *SHEPARD'S*

In researching defamation, you encounter a 9th Circuit case called *Masson v. New Yorker*. The cite is 895 F.2d 1535. You want to Shepardize it to see if it is still good law and to find authority from a particular circuit.

1.   How many *Shepard's* volumes do you need to consult to comprehensively Shepardize the case?

2.   Give a citation to a 6th Circuit case citing Masson.

3.   Has Masson been reversed or overruled? If so, give the citation to the case (use Blue Book form).

◆Using your impeccable research skills, you found a case very similar factually to the Sheriff John Brown incident. It is a New Hampshire case titled McCusker v. Valley News, 121 N.H. 258, 428 A.2d 493 (197?). You want to see if it has been cited by a law review or other secondary authority.

4.   What *Shepard's* volumes should you look in?

5.   How many *Shepard's* volumes do you need to consult to comprehensively Shepardize the case?

6.   Give the citation to a law review article citing McCusker.

◆Now you want to see if there are cases from states other than New Hampshire that have cited

McCusker. After all, these might also be concerning sheriffs as public figures or public officials.

7.   What *Shepard's* volumes should you look in?

8.   How many *Shepard's* volumes do you need to consult to comprehensively Shepardize the case?

9.   How many states (other than New Hampshire) have decisions citing *McCusker*? What states are they?

◆Besides finding authority from other states, *Shepard's* allows you to focus in on a particular headnote.

10.   Using the same volumes you just used, are there any cases (in any jurisdiction) citing *McCusker* for the proposition stated in headnote 3 of the Atlantic Reporter version of the case? If so, give the citation(s).

◆*Shepard's* can also be useful in guiding you to decisions that may be most helpful in interpreting a case. This is the function of the analysis abbreviations of certain citing cases.

11.   Are there any cases that "explain" the holding in *McCusker*?

◆Recall the administrative regulations of an earlier exercise. The bicycle safety regulations were found at 16 CFR 1512. If you want to find cases citing this regulation, you use *Shepard's*.

12.   What *Shepard's* volumes do you use to find cases citing federal administrative regulations?

13.   How many volumes must you consult to comprehensively shepardize this regulation.

14.   Has the regulation ever been found unconstitutional? If so, give the citation(s) of the case(s) finding it so.

✦Find the *Shepard's* for Restatements.

15.   Give the citation to a Hawaii case citing Restatement of Contracts, Second §229.

Chapter 17
Computer-Assisted Legal Research

◆**EXERCISE 17.A - COMPUTER-ASSISTED LEGAL RESEARCH**

Your client, Norman, was walking to the Regal Beagle lounge last winter. In front of the house of one Chrissy, Norman slipped on some ice or snow and fell, injuring his back. You have been assigned to find out if Norman has a cause of action against either Chrissy or the city. Do the research in your home state.

◆Select either LEXIS or WESTLAW. Run a search or searches on the selected system to find authority on the issue.

1.   What database or file did you choose to run your search in?

2.   What was the search you used (show exactly what you typed into the computer)?

3.   How many documents did you retrieve?

4.   If you had to change or modify the search, what is the full search that you ultimately used?

◆Browse through several of the documents looking for your search terms.

5.   Give the cite to a case that appears to be on point.

6.   Shepardize or Keycite (only available on WESTLAW) the above case (notice that the computer cumulates all volumes of Shepard's). Give the citation to a case that cites the case.

✦Go back to or resume the original database or file. Run a new search using "fields" or "segments." Find a California case on the death penalty decided by Justice Lucas after 1994 (First make sure you are in the California database or file; then use the "judge" or "opinionby" field or segment along with your search on the death penalty; last, add the date limitation. Again use a field or segment.).

7.   Give the citation to a case you found.

✦When you sign off, notice the amount of time you have spent online. Sign off.

8.   How much time were you online?

✦To give you a rough equivalent for how much the online time would have cost you at commercial rates, multiply the number of minutes you spent online by $4.00.

9.   How much would your online search have cost?

10.   Do you think you spent less time online solving the first problem than you would have using conventional resources?

11.   Do you think you found documents that you would not have found using conventional resources?

✦It is difficult to generalize about when computers should and should not be used. Or rather, when they are more efficient. The competing factors are the amount of time they save you versus the additional costs they entail. Notice, however, that for certain problems like the problem of finding opinions by Justice Lucas, the computer may be the only solution (this task is virtually impossible using conventional resources). The lesson to be learned from this is to look beyond a book mentality when using the computer. Don't ask if it can do what a book can do. Instead, ask yourself what your client's information needs are and then ask if the computer can somehow be manipulated to retrieve that information.

✦EXERCISE 17.B - USE OF INTERNET

1. Choose an Internet browser (e.g., Netscape Navigator or Microsoft Explorer). List your choice here.

2. From the Internet browser, choose one of the "web guides" (for example, Yahoo). Follow the string of topics and subtopics to find the United States House of Representatives home page. Keep track of what links you click on and list them below.

3. What is the URL for Thomas (the House of Representative's page for legislative information on the Internet)?

4. Return back to your home page. There should be a button to click on that allows you to do this in one step. This time, choose one of the search engines (such as Alta Vista). If you are unfamiliar with the search engine, you might want to look at the search help information (note that the help button will be the one on the page rather than the one on the browser). Enter a search into the search box to find the United States House of Representatives Thomas database. Show what search terms and protocols you used below.

5. Look through the web pages retrieved to find Thomas or a link to Thomas. Make a bookmark for the Thomas home page. Return to your home page and then access Thomas by using the bookmark. Did the process work?

6. Try to locate the home page for your state government. Use whatever approach works best for you. What is the URL (web address)?

7. Browse the state government web site to find judicial opinions from the state's highest court. If you find them, can you determine how far back the opinions go? If so, give that information.

8. Click on the "Open" button. Remember, you can use this when you want to access a web site that you already have the URL for. Type in:

    www.whitehouse.gov

    Leave a message if you feel so inclined. Name three links that this page allows you to access.

Chapter 18
How To Approach a Legal Research Problem

✦EXERCISE 18.A - SELECTING THE APPROPRIATE RESOURCE

In the following questions, if you decide that online resources are appropriate, identify the database or file and the search that you would enter.

1.   Your supervising attorney knows of a case decided "in the last year or so in some western state" finding a curfew ordinance unconstitutionally vague and overbroad. What resource(s) would you begin with and why?

2.   You are asked to research franchising a business. You know very little about what franchising is, much less what laws govern it. What resource(s) would you begin your research with and why?

3.   Your supervising attorney gives you a federal statute and asks you how a phrase in it has been applied. What resource(s) would you begin with and why?

4.   Your client wants a power of attorney drawn that becomes operative only upon her incapacity. What resource(s) would you begin your research with and why?

5.   Your supervising attorney asks you to find any cases you can discussing an over-the-counter headache medicine called *Throb-B-Gone*. Its chemical name is benzacortiprednizone. What resource(s) would you begin your research with and why?

6.   Your supervising attorney has a federal case. She wants you to find cases from your home state that discuss one of the issues in the case. What resource(s) would you begin your

Writing
Exercises
◆◆◆

✦**EXERCISE 21.A - PARAGRAPH LENGTH**

This exercise should be done after reading Section 21.4 in the *Handbook*.

✦Read the following paragraph from an appellate brief and decide if it should be broken up into shorter paragraphs and, if so, where.

There are some limited exceptions to the prohibitive rule stated in the above cases; however, the facts of the instant case do not fall into those exceptions. The first exception allows the questioning of a witness about religious beliefs when those beliefs are relevant to some issue other than the credibility of the witness. *State v. Stone*, 728 P.2d 674 (Ariz. Ct. App. 1986). In the instant case, Ms. Patten's religious activities and beliefs were not at issue and the only conceivable purpose that the prosecution could have had for questioning her about them was to bolster her credibility by impressing the jury with her religiousness. The second exception applies when reference to the religious beliefs of a witness is isolated and not significant to the trial proceedings in their entirety. *Id*. at 871, 728 P.2d at 678. In the instant case, the prosecution's questions--over repeated objections--about Ms. Patten's religious beliefs, as well as the closing argument comments about those beliefs, cannot be deemed isolated and inadvertent. (RP 151-52, 186). Under the third exception, inquiry about the religious beliefs of a witness will not give rise to constitutional error if the assigning party invites the error. *People v. Baseer*, 90 Ill. App. 3d 866, 414 N.E.2d 5 (1980). Hence, when a defendant testifies as to his own religious beliefs in an attempt to bolster his credibility, he will not be heard to complain when the prosecution cross-examines him about his beliefs. *Id.* at 871, 414 N.E.2d at 10. In the instant case, Mr. Davidson's counsel never attempted to question Ms. Patten about her religious beliefs so as to affect her credibility, so it cannot be said that the defense "opened the door" to the prosecution's questioning of Ms. Patten about her religious beliefs. *Id.* In short, none of the exceptions apply. Therefore, the trial court's allowance of the prosecution's questioning was an error of constitutional magnitude.

✦EXERCISE 21.B - PARAGRAPH LENGTH

This exercise should be done after reading Section 21.4 in the *Handbook*.

✦Read the following statement of facts and decide if the paragraphs are the appropriate length. Rewrite and re-paragraph as needed.

Statement of Facts

Despite several neighbors' complaints, the Metropolitan School Board has allowed Say No to Drugs (SND) baseball games to be played at Urban High on Tuesday and Thursday from 8 p.m. to midnight. The SND program, aimed at local drug users, has been very successful and has attracted nationwide attention. Four neighbors living adjacent to the Urban High athletic field--Mr. and Mrs. Archer, Mr. Baker, Mr. and Mrs. Carlisle, and Mrs. DeLeon--have filed suit against the school district in Washington State Superior Court, Puget Sound County. These neighbors seek to enjoin baseball at Urban High between the hours of 9:30 p.m. and midnight. They also seek monetary compensation for damages resulting from nuisance and trespass.

Mr. and Mrs. Archer, an elderly couple, compete in growing roses. Before September 1987, the Archers had approximately 20 rosebushes, most of which were budding. Since September, four of their bushes have been destroyed. In addition, so many buds have been damaged that the Archers will be unable to enter any rose competitions this season. The Archers allege that baseball players trespassing across their property have caused the damage.

Mr. Baker, a night court judge who works from 5 p.m. to 1 a.m., has had two picture windows and a valuable vase broken by baseballs.

The Carlisles are a young couple with an 18-month-old daughter. The lights and noise from the night baseball prevent their daughter from sleeping until 12:30 a.m. Although these disturbances to her sleep occur only twice a week, the Carlisles claim that the loss of sleep interrupts the baby's entire weekly schedule.

Mrs. DeLeon, a stockbroker, wakes at 5 a.m. to be at work by 7 a.m. Lately, she has been irritable at work. Her job performance has suffered, and tranquilizers have not helped. Mrs. DeLeon alleges her problem is her inability to sleep because of the lights and noise from the night baseball. She claims that if the night baseball continues, she will have to sell her home at a loss.

No baseballs or baseball players have entered the Carlisles' or Mrs. DeLeon's property. Both the Carlisles' and Mrs. DeLeon's property are protected by a high fence, but the school property itself is not fenced between the plaintiffs' property and the field.

Urban High's field is the only lighted baseball field within a ten-mile radius of Urban High.

✦EXERCISE 21.C - TOPIC SENTENCES

This exercise should be done after reading Section 21.5.1 in the *Handbook*.

✦Read the following paragraphs and revise the topic sentences so that they 1) transition from the preceding paragraph, 2) introduce the new topic, and 3) assert something about the new topic.

1.   Even though the more current cases adopt a liberal reading, there are cases that support a motion to quash service. These cases limit *Rovinski* by recognizing that "it is not enough to have actual notice. In *Frasca*, for example, service of process was left with defendant's daughter-in-law in Pennsylvania. The defendant, who did receive actual notice, had lived in Massachusetts for fifty years and had visited his son in Pennsylvania only twice during that time. *Id.* at 269.

2.   In order to use *Frasca* to support our client, we must characterize Ms. Clay-Poole's trips to California as visits. She stayed only three or four days at a time. The possessions she kept in California were not enough for even a three or four day visit, so she had to carry additional belongings with her. By demonstrating that her contacts with the California

residence were minimal, we can show that her husband's home was not her "dwelling house or usual place of abode."

3.   The plaintiff will point out the factual differences between our case and *Frasca*. Frasca was clearly a visitor in Pennsylvania. He apparently did not travel there with any regularity. He had only been at the house two times in the past fifty years. Our client travels to California regularly, keeps clothing at the house, and receives mail addressed to her and her husband there. Her contacts are more extensive.

4.   Concerning element number one, was Smith a member of the ADEA protected class at the time of his discharge? At the time of Smith's discharge, ADEA applied only to individuals who were at least forty years old but less than seventy years old. 29 U.S.C. §631(a) (1982). Because Smith was forty-nine years old when he was discharged, he was within the ADEA protected class. Therefore, element number one is satisfied.

✦EXERCISE 21.D - TOPIC AND CONCLUDING SENTENCES

This exercise should be done after reading Section 21.5.2 in the *Handbook.*

✦Find the topic sentence and concluding sentence in the following paragraph. Discuss whether the topic sentence signals to the reader the key point that the paragraph will make and whether the concluding sentence is helpful to the reader.

A good illustration of the court awarding damages for inconvenience and annoyance is *Riblet v. Spokane-Portland Cement Co.*, 45 Wash. 2d 346, 274 P.2d 574 (1954). In *Riblet*, the plaintiffs were able to recover for the annoyance and inconvenience caused by cement dust. Although the dust itself was imperceptible "as is usually the case when nuisance involves dust, gas, smoke, noise, etc.," the dust's effects disrupted the ordinary activities of family life. Consequently, the annoyance was compensable. *Id.*

✦EXERCISE 21.E - PARAGRAPH BLOCKS

This exercise should be done after reading Section 21.6 in the *Handbook.*

✦Read the following discussion section of a memo. Mark the topic paragraphs for paragraph blocks and the topic sentences for individual paragraphs.

Discussion

"Actual physical control" is governed by a statute that states in part: "It is unlawful . . . for any person who is under the influence of alcohol to . . . be in actual physical control of a motor vehicle upon the ways of this state open to the public." Mont. Code Ann. §61.8.4011)(a) (1983). Generally, three elements of the statute bear examination: 1) the person must be under the influence of alcohol; 2) the person must be in actual physical control of a motor vehicle; and 3) the motor vehicle must be on the ways of Montana that are open to the public.

Under the Influence_

Considering the fact pattern of the Renko case, the court will probably find that the question of whether Mr. Renko was under the influence of alcohol is not worthy of in-depth discussion. The results of the breathalyzer test, the vomit, and the testimony of the arresting officer establish that our client was legally intoxicated at the time of arrest, so the first element of the offense is not at issue.

Ways of the State

Although the primary issue of the case focuses upon resolving questions pertaining to actual physical control, the issue of whether Mr. Renko's truck was on the ways of the state open to the public deserves brief analysis. The traffic code states that "'ways of the state open to the public' means any highway, road, alley lane, parking area, or other public or private place adapted and fitted for public travel that is in common use by the public." Mont. Code Ann. §61.8.101(1)(1983). The language specifically states "adapted and fitted for public travel." Since Mr. Renko's truck was found on the shoulder, the court would have to determine whether the shoulder of a highway is adapted and fitted for public travel. In defining other statutory language, the Montana Supreme Court resorted to dictionary definitions. Webster defines shoulder as "either edge of a roadway; specifically: the part of the roadway *outside the traveled way*" (emphasis added). It is possible, then, that the court could interpret the statutory language narrowly and conclude that the term "ways" does not encompass shoulders.

However, a narrow construction of the term "ways" is unlikely. In fact, there are two strong indications that Montana will favor a broad construction: 1) an extension stated in the statutory definition of "highway"; and 2) an interpretation of "ways" given in a Montana Supreme Court decision. By statutory definition, "[h]ighway means the entire width between the boundary lines of every publicly maintained way when any part thereof is open to the use of the public for purposes of vehicular travel, *except that for the purpose of chapter 8 the term also includes ways which have been or shall be dedicated to public use*." (emphasis added) Mont. Code Ann. §61.1.201 (1983). Chapter 8 includes offenses committed while under the influence of alcohol. Since the legislature expanded the statutory definition for alcohol-related offenses, it follows that the legislature intended to broaden, not narrow, the term. Following the legislature's lead, the Montana Supreme Court stipulated that "ways" encompasses state and county right-of-ways, including borrow pits, which road maintenance crews use as sources of dirt and gravel. *State v. Taylor,* 242 Mont. 43, 44, 661 P.2d 33, 34 (1983). It is highly unlikely that the court would include borrow pits but exempt shoulders from the term "ways." The court will probably conclude that Mr. Renko's truck was on the ways of the state open to the public.

Actual Physical Control

Although it is relatively easy to determine that the facts in this case satisfy the elements of "under the influence" and "on the ways," it is more difficult to decide whether they constitute "actual physical control" of a motor vehicle. The statute does not further explain "actual physical control," but the Montana Supreme Court supplied the following dictionary definition: "[I]t means existing or present bodily restraint, directing influence, domination or regulation of an automobile." *State v. Ruona*, 133 Mont. 243,

246, 321 P.2d 615, 618 (1958).

The elements of the definition have not been completely defined; however, the court has given some clarification. In *Ruona*, the court stated that "restraint" includes preventing a car from moving; movement of a vehicle is not necessary for actual physical control. 133 Mont. at 246, 321 P.2d at 618. The court further clarified the term "regulation" by asserting that a sleeping driver who remains behind the steering wheel of a vehicle "remains in a position to regulate" the vehicle and "has not relinquished control" of the vehicle. *Taylor*, 242 Mont. at 44, 661 P.2d 34. Regulation or control is not diminished by the fact that a vehicle is incapable of moving because, as previously noted, movement is not required. *Taylor*, 242 Mont. at 44, 661 P.2d at 34 (citing *Ruona*, 133 Mont. at 247, 321 P.2d at 619).

The Montana court has applied these definitions to cases with the following fact patterns: 1) the driver was asleep and intoxicated; 2) the driver was positioned behind the steering wheel of the motor vehicle; 3) the vehicle's motor was running; 4) the vehicle was parked; and 5) the vehicle was at least partially on the pavement of a roadway. In both of the leading Montana cases, the court held that the driver was in actual physical control of his vehicle. *Ruona*, 133 Mont. 243, 321 P.2d 615; *Taylor*, 242 Mont. 43, 661 P.2d 33. However, the court has not addressed the exact fact pattern presented by the Renko case.

The Renko fact pattern differs in the following respects: 1) the driver was not

seated behind the steering wheel; 2) the engine of the vehicle was not running; and 3) the

vehicle was not even partially on the traveled portion of the roadway. Although the

"driver's position" may be considered separately, "engine not running" and "vehicle not

on roadway" are closely related in terms of legal significance and should be analyzed

together. In fact, the interrelationship of all three factors should be considered for two

reasons. First, although a single factor may not affect the outcome of a case, the

combination of that factor with others may be legally significant. Second, the

combination of the aforementioned factors may be important in showing the defendant's

intent.

Positioning in the driver's seat is a common element in all the national cases that

have found actual physical control of a motionless vehicle, *State v. Smelter*, 36 Wash.

App. 439, 441, 674 P.2d 690, 692 (1984), except for one Oklahoma case, *Hughes v. State*,

509 Okla., 157, 535 P.2d 1023 (1975) (Defendant was lying across the front seat but was

awake and the vehicle was not only on the roadway but also at a 90 degree angle to the

flow of traffic.) The theory behind the decisions is that an intoxicated person who is

seated behind the steering wheel is still in a position to control the vehicle and could be

considered a potential threat to the public. *Ruona*, 133 Mont. at 243, 321 P.2d at 619

(quoting *State v. Webb*, 78 Ariz. 8, 274 P.2d 338, (1954)).

The Montana court could view the positioning question in two ways: 1) it could hold that positioning behind the steering wheel is essential to manifest control of the vehicle, *Cincinnati v. Kelley*, 47 Ohio St. 2d 94, 351 N.E.2d 85 (1976); or 2) it could find that positioning is relatively unimportant because once awakened, a driver could quickly move behind the wheel and would pose as great a threat to society as the driver who remained behind the wheel while he slept. *State v. Bugger,* 25 Utah 2d 404, 483 P.2d 442, (1971) (Ellett, J., dissenting). Considering that the Montana court has focused on the idea that the purpose of the statute is to protect the public and has found that a sleeping, intoxicated driver is still a threat to the public, *Ruona*, 133 Mont. at 243, 321 P.2d at 619, the court would probably find that a sleeping, intoxicated driver who is lying on the front seat poses a potential threat to the public.

Because only a few cases have addressed the issues of whether actual physical control of a vehicle can be established when the engine is not running or when the vehicle is entirely off the traveled portion of the roadway, it is difficult to isolate these factors in terms of legal significance. Actual physical control has been found when the vehicle was legally parked and the engine was not running but when the driver was awake and in the driver's seat. *Kelley*, 47 Ohio St. 2d 94, 351 N.E.2d 85. In *Kelley*, the court noted that the defendant was behind the wheel, had possession of the key, and was in such a condition that he could have started the vehicle. 47 Ohio St. 2d 94, 351 N.E.2d 85.

In contrast, courts have been reluctant to find actual physical control when the driver has been found asleep in a vehicle that was legally parked on the shoulder of the

45

roadway with the engine turned off. For example, in *State v. Bugger*, the Utah Supreme

Court held that a defendant was not in actual physical control because he was not

controlling the vehicle or exercising any dominion over it. *State v. Bugger*, 25 Utah 2d

404, 483 P.2d 442. In *State v. Zavala*, the Arizona Supreme Court held that a defendant

had voluntarily relinquished control of the vehicle. *State v. Zavala*, 136 Ariz. 356, 666

P.2d 456 (1983). The Arizona court considered the voluntary action or intent of the

driver important and wished to foster the policy of encouraging drunk drivers to pull out

of traffic, to turn off the engine, and to go to sleep. *Zavala*, 136 Ariz. 356, 666 P.2d 456

(1983).

In short, before the Montana court can determine whether Mr. Renko was in

actual physical control of the vehicle, the court must determine the following issues: 1)

whether Mr. Renko had relinquished control of the vehicle; and 2) whether the Montana

legislature intended to foster a policy of encouraging intoxicated drivers to pull off the

road to sleep.

With regard to the first issue, other jurisdictions have partially defined "control"

and "operate" in terms of the defendant's manipulation of mechanical or electrical

apparatus. Cases that relate to such a definition have dealt with defendants who were

awake and were attempting either to brake or to steer inoperable vehicles. *State v. Swift*,

125 Conn. 399, 6 A.2d 359 (1939); *State v. Storrs*, 105 Vt. 180, 163 A. 56 (1933).

However, it is conceivable that a court, particularly one that is inclined to broadly construe traffic regulations concerning intoxicated drivers, could apply the "manipulation of mechanical and electrical apparatus" definition in the Renko case. The court could conclude that Mr. Renko's left foot was manipulating the brake pedal and illuminating the brake lights; therefore, he had not relinquished control of the vehicle. The court could reach the same conclusion by finding that Mr. Renko was using "present bodily restraint" to prevent the car from moving.

As a subissue in determining control, the court would have to address the question of whether operability is required. If it is not required, then no further discussion of this issue would be necessary; and in light of the Montana court's holding in *Taylor*, operability probably would not be required because movement is not required and the driver was still considered to be in actual physical control of a vehicle that he could not move. 242 Mont. at 43, 661 P.2d at 34.

If some form of operability is required, then the court must decide whether to focus on the defendant's ability to operate the vehicle or on the vehicle's condition. *State v. Smelter*, 36 Wash. App. 439, 444, 674 P.2d 690, 693 (1984). In focusing on the defendant's condition, the court could find that since the defendant had the key and was in the cab of the truck, he would have been able to operate the vehicle had he been awakened. Not only is it possible that he could have operated the truck, it is evident that he did drive the truck from the tavern to the freeway before parking it on the shoulder. In focusing on the vehicle's condition, the Washington court used the trial court's "reasonably operable" standard and defined that term as any malfunction short of a cracked block or a similar problem that would render the vehicle totally inoperable. *Smelter*, 36 Wash. App. at 444, 674 P.2d at 693. By that definition, Mr. Renko's truck was reasonably operable regardless of whether it would start. Therefore, if the Montana court considers operability an issue, it would probably find that Mr. Renko was capable of operating the vehicle and that the vehicle was in reasonably operable condition.

The second question, whether the legislature wishes to foster a policy of encouraging intoxicated drivers to pull off the road to sleep, includes considering the importance of the defendant's intent. Intent and policy an be looked at in two ways. The first, that presented by the Arizona court in *Zavala*, is that the driver who realizes that he is not in condition to drive and pulls off the roadway to sleep should be rewarded. If the court were not to reward such behavior, then the driver would be tempted to proceed to his destination and would present a greater threat to public safety. 136 Ariz. 356, 666 P.2d 456. The second view is that the drunken driver not only intended to drive but also did drive his car from the tavern to the freeway, and it is better policy to encourage an intoxicated person to avoid driving in the first place. In accord with this view, the Washington court noted that statutes prohibiting driving while intoxicated are primarily preventive measures that are designed to deter intoxicated persons from entering vehicles except as passengers. *Smelter*, 36 Wash. App. at 444, 674 P.2d at 693 (citing *State v. Ghylin*, 250 N.W.2d 252, 255 (N.D. 1977)). The *Smelter* court agreed with other courts that have held that such legislation should be liberally interpreted with the effect of

48

promoting the public interest at the expense of the private interest of the inebriated driver. 36 Wash. App. at 444, 674 P.2d at 693.

Recent statutory revisions in Montana seem to follow this line of reasoning. The Montana legislature revised the traffic code in 1983 and purposely broadened the scope of the laws relating to drunken drivers. The intent was to allow patrol officers to apprehend drunken drivers before such drivers could create accidents. *Montana's Legislative Attempt to Deal with the Drinking Driver: The 1983 DWI Statutes*, 46 Mont. L. Rev. 315 (1985). The Montana court followed suit in *Taylor* by liberally construing the statutes. 242 Mont. 43, 661 P.2d 33. Considering the legislative intent and the court's demonstrated tendencies toward liberal construction, the court will probably side with Justice Ellett, who dissented in *Bugger:*

It does not matter whether the motor is running or is idle nor whether the drunk is in the front seat or in the back seat. His potentiality for harm is lessened but not obviated by a silent motor or a backseat position--provided, of course, that he is the one in control of the car. It only takes a flick of the wrist to start the motor or to engage the gears, and it requires only a moment of time to get under the wheel from the back seat. A drunk in control of a motor vehicle has such a propensity to cause harm that the statute intended to make it criminal for him to be in a position to do so. *State v. Bugger*, 25 Utah 2d 404, 405, 483 P.2d 442, 443 (1971) (Ellett, J., dissenting).

Conclusion

The Montana court will probably find that Andrew Renko was in actual physical control of a motor vehicle while intoxicated. Although it would be unprecedented to find "actual physical control" when the person was asleep across the front seat and the engine was not running, the Montana court has not been reluctant to break new ground. The court was a leader in defining "actual physical control," and many jurisdictions have followed the Montana definition.

Focusing on the threat to the public, the Montana legislature broadened the statutes to make it easier to apprehend intoxicated individuals before they cause motor vehicle accidents. The Montana court followed suit by broadly construing statutory wording. The tendency in Montana is toward an expanded definition. Therefore, it would be inconsistent for the court to conclude that Mr. Renko was not in actual physical control of his vehicle.

✦EXERCISE 21.F - PARAGRAPH BLOCKS

This exercise should be done after reading Section 21.6 in the *Handbook*.

✦Mark the concluding paragraphs for paragraph blocks and the concluding sentences for individual paragraphs for the discussion section of the memo in Exercise 20.E.

✦Exercise 21.G - Paragraph Length

This exercise should be done after reading Section 21.6 in the *Handbook*.

✦Examine the length of the paragraphs on the memo in Exercise 20.E. Are any paragraphs too long? Too short? Where would you add or take out paragraph breaks? Does the one-sentence paragraph ("In short, before the Montana court . . . ") work? If so, why? If not, why not?

Chapter 22
Connections Between Sentences

♦**EXERCISE 22.A - GENERIC TRANSITIONS**

This exercise should be done after reading Section 22.1 in the *Handbook*.

♦Generic transitions include those words and phrases that are used in every kind of writing; consequently, they are familiar to all readers and writers.

The following are the most common generic transitions grouped by function.

For Contrast

however	nevertheless*	but
on the other hand	conversely	still
by (in) contrast	notwithstanding	yet
on the contrary	nonetheless*	instead
contrary to _____	alternatively	though
unlike _____	even so*	although
despite _____	rather	even
		though

---

* Generic transition that falls under more than one category.

53

For Comparison

similarly	analogously	in like
likewise	in the same way	manner
	for the same reason	

For Cause and Effect

therefore*	accordingly	hence
consequently*	thus*	since
as a result	because	so
		for

For Addition

also	moreover	besides
further	too	in addition
furthermore	additionally	and

For Examples

for example	to illustrate	specifically
for instance	namely	that is*

---

* Generic transition that falls under more than one category.

For Emphasis

in fact	certainly	still*
above all	indeed	clearly

For Evaluation

more importantly	surprisingly	unquestioningly
unfortunately	allegedly	
fortunately	arguably	

For Restatement

in other words	more simply	to put it differently
that is*	simply put	

For Concession

granted	of course	to be sure

For Resumption After a Concession

still*	nonetheless*	all the same
nevertheless*	even so*	

For Time

subsequently	later	earlier
recently	eventually	afterwards

---

*Generic transition that falls under more than one category.

meanwhile	shortly thereafter	until now
initially	simultaneously	since
formerly	at the time	

For Place

| adjacent to | here | nearby |
| next to | beyond | opposite to |

For Sequence

first, second, third	next	then
former, latter	final	later
in the first place	finally*	primary,
		secondary

For Conclusion

in summary	in brief	thus*
in sum	in short	therefore*
to sum up	to conclude	consequently*
finally*	in conclusion	to (in)
	review	

---

*Generic Transition that falls under more than one category.

◆Each of the following pairs or sequences of sentences requires a generic transition to show the connection between the ideas. Select an appropriate generic transition and place it at the point of connection.

1.   For ten years Mr. Hillary has owned a restaurant located on Puget Sound in Tacoma, Washington. Mr. Sam Wry owns the adjoining business, the Fitness Club, which has operated for one year. Mr. Hillary has become annoyed by the shop patrons wearing skimpy bathing suits during the aerobics class on the Fitness Club's lawn within full view of restaurant customers.

2.   Wry has satisfied all necessary zoning and licensing requirements. He has legally opened the Fitness Club in the community.

3.   Hillary will claim that the entire community is offended by the skimpy bathing suits and the loud raucous behavior at the Fitness Club. Hillary will claim that he is specially injured because he is losing the income from those patrons who will no longer eat at his restaurant.

4.   In a 1964 opinion, the Court stated that just because "a thing is unsightly or offends the aesthetic sense of a neighbor does not ordinarily make it a nuisance or afford ground for injunctive relief." *Mathewson v. Primeau*, 64 Wash. 2d 929, 938, 395 P.2d 183, 189 (1964). The fact that some people were offended by activities at the Fitness Shop does not furnish a valid basis for a nuisance action.

5.   The fundamental inquiry is whether the use of the property is reasonable or unreasonable. *Morin v. Johnson*, 49 Wash. 2d at 280, 300 P.2d at 571 (1956). The use must unreasonably interfere with another's use and enjoyment of property.

6.   In *Turtle*, the court enjoined the establishment of a lakefront resort on the grounds that management would be unable to control the patrons, that the privacy of the neighboring residents would be disturbed, and that such a resort was alien to the character of the neighborhood. *Turtle v. Fitchett*, 156 Wash. 328, 287 P. 7 (1930). Hillary may argue that the Fitness Club has failed to control the aerobics classes, as evidenced by the noise, that the established sedate environment in the restaurant has been disrupted, and that the Fitness Club's activities are alien to the refined and tastefully commercial nature of the locale.

7.   Washington courts do not determine nuisance by subjective values. The presence of nuisance is evaluated in objective terms.

8.   If the elements are not met, the plaintiff could not maintain an action for public nuisance. He could consider a cause of action for private nuisance.

9.   In finding that a public beach and camp are not a public nuisance, the court found these points compelling. The noise complained of was "ordinary." *Hayes*, 311. It came from

58

people behaving "in an orderly manner." *Id.* No intoxicants were sold or permitted on the beach. *Id.* at 313. The activities did not affect the rights of the entire neighborhood equally. *Id.*

10.   In *Hayes*, the court found that neighbors suffered some occasional minor annoyance from the beach's patrons but that such annoyances were not extraordinary or unusual from a group of people gathered for recreation. The court found that the noise and activity were insufficient to support a cause of action for nuisance.

✦EXERCISE 22.B - DOVETAILING

This exercise should be done after reading Section 22.3 in the *Handbook*.

Dovetailing. Dovetailing is the overlap of language between two sentences that creates a bridge between those two sentences. Dovetails are often created by moving the connecting idea to the end of the first sentence and the beginning of the second sentence, repeating key words, using pronouns to refer back to nouns an earlier sentence, and using "hook words" (this, that, these, such) and a summarizing noun.

✦Revise the following sentences by using the dovetailing technique.

1.   An official of the Justice Department asked Conan to inform him of any activities of Congressman Lemming that might be politically embarrassing. The Justice Department offered him a reward.

59

2. Conan had no personal motive for his actions. He assisted the Justice Department in order to receive a reward.

3. Washington courts have held that the State can be liable for actions that are operational. Discretionary, planning, and design actions are not included.

4. Operational acts are ministerial acts that are performed by agents in accordance with the criteria set up by the State. The agents do not exercise their own judgment.

5. Mr. Pugh took financial log books from Mr. Snowadzki's private desk, copied them, and delivered them to the IRS. The IRS examined Mr. Snowadzki's tax returns, and he was subsequently tried and convicted on two counts of filing false tax returns.

6. In 1983, the Montana legislature adopted new and stricter laws to deal with drunk drivers. The jurisdiction of law enforcement was extended and faster and stiffer penalties were provided.

7. In Montana, a highway is defined by statute as "the entire width between the boundary lines of every publicly maintained way . . . ." Mont. Code Ann. §61-1-201 (1976). Not specifically addressed is the shoulder of the highway.

8. One of the Montana cases dealt with a vehicle that was stuck in a borrow pit off the roadway. The court interpreted the statutory definition of highway to include the burrow pit.

9. Unfortunately, there are not any cases in which a conviction was overturned based solely on the motorist's position in the vehicle. The court will probably not consider the position of Mr. Renko's head or body to be a significant factor.

10. The policy underlying the family car doctrine favors the Whites' position. Victims who have been injured by the negligent driving of minors should be compensated.

✦EXERCISE 22.C - DOVETAILING

This exercise should be done after reading Section 22.3 in the *Handbook*.

✦The following paragraphs are choppy. Revise using the dovetailing technique.

1.   On December 4, 1986, Mrs. Clive White, who was then five and a half months pregnant, was driving through an intersection when her car was struck by a car driven by seventeen-year-old Randy Thompson. Mrs. Pettus was thrown against the dashboard and against the passenger side of the car. Mrs. White gave birth to a stillborn child that same night. Mrs. White is suffering severe emotional distress.

2.   A foreseeable risk, one which public official knew of or should have known of, can be established through objective evidence. Injuries incurred by plaintiffs in similar situations would be an example. A jury would determine the foreseeability of the harm that the defendant had a duty to reasonably guard.

✦The following paragraph is somewhat disjointed because the writer violated the old --> new principle in spots. Revise accordingly.

3.   In October 1986, the Governor formed a panel of experts to study the daycare service crisis. Panel members visited daycare facilities throughout the state and wrote a report on their findings. The Governor, by Executive Order, initiated a daycare facility program inspection after conferring with panel members and considering their report. Pursuant to the order, the Secretary of State Department of Social and Health Services studied the panel's report, developed a set of inspection criteria, and circulated the criteria via interdepartmental memorandum. The inspectors were directed by the memorandum to consider seven factors.

✦EXERCISE 22.D - ALL TRANSITIONS

This exercise should be done after reading Section 22.3 in the *Handbook*.

✦Read the following statement of facts from a memorandum. Underline the instances where dovetailing is used and circle the generic and orienting transitions. In the instances where dovetailing is not used, explain why.

STATEMENT OF FACTS

Mr. and Mrs. Abernathy, our clients, live in a mobile home park near Vancouver, Washington. Because Vancouver is located in Clark County, just across the Columbia River from Portland, Oregon, it is rapidly becoming a "bedroom community" for the metropolitan Portland area.

In 1979, Clark County enacted a mobile home park ordinance. The County passed the ordinance in response to the concerns of mobile home owners over the scarcity of mobile home spaces in the area and the tight restrictions on the use of rural land. Mobile home regulation is also covered by the Washington State Mobile Home Landlord-Tenant Act, passed by the legislature in 1977.

In October 1983, the Abernathys' landlord, Frank C. Johnson, informed them that, because of his increased operating express, he planned to raise their monthly rent from $275 to $500, effective January 1, 1984. The Abernathys' year-to-year lease expired at that time, and a renewal of the lease was contingent on their agreement to the rent increase.

On October 31, 1983, the Abernathys wrote to Mr. Johnson requesting arbitration as provided for in the county ordinance. The provision allows a mobile home owner presented with a lease or rental fee increase to petition for public fact-finding by an arbitrator to determine whether the proposed rate is reasonable. Mr. Johnson did not respond to the Abernathys' request.

On January 1, 1984, Mr. Johnson notified the Abernathys that they had failed to execute a lease. Therefore, they were to vacate the premises before February 29, 1984. The Abernathys refuse to leave.

Recently, Mr. Johnson filed an unlawful detainer action against the Abernathys. Among the claims is the assertion that the Clark County ordinance violates the taking provision of the

Washington State Constitution and United States Constitution.

The Abernathys do not wish to vacate their trailer space. They have asked whether the landlord acted properly when he raised their rent and when he sent them their termination notice. In addition, they want to know what rights and remedies they have under the state statute and the county ordinance.

✦EXERCISE 22.E - ALL TRANSITIONS

This exercise should be done after reading Section 22.3 in the *Handbook*.

✦The following excerpt from the rules section of the same memorandum has problems with dovetailing and transitions. Revise to provide strong connections between the sentences.

Any county, city, town, or township may make and enforce within its limits all such local police, sanitary, and other regulations that do not conflict with general laws. Wash. Const. Art. 11, §11 (1964). Unless there is room for concurrent jurisdiction, the power of a municipality to regulate a particular subject ceases when the state enacts a general law on that subject. *Lenci v. City of Seattle*, 63 Wash. 2d 664, 669, 388 P.2d 926, 930 (1964). So long as its enactments do not conflict with the state legislation, a municipality may enact local legislation upon subjects already covered by state legislation. *Id.* at 670, 388 P.2d at 931.

Nevertheless, the Washington Supreme Court has set out two tests to determine whether a local ordinance was "in conflict" with--and therefore preempted by--a state statute. There would be no room for concurrent jurisdiction, if the state legislature's intent in enacting a statute was to completely occupy a given field of regulation, thereby preempting any local ordinance by the statute. *Id.* at 669, 388 P.2d at 930. If the express provisions of a local ordinance and of a state statute are in such direct conflict that they cannot be reconciled, the statute would prevail. *Id.* at 670, 388 P.2d at 931.

The Washington State Legislature had enacted a general law covering the regulation of mobile homes. Wash. Rev. Code ch. 59.20 (1977). The Clark County Ordinance 79-801 covering the same subject would be preempted in its entirety if the legislature's intent in enacting the statute was to completely occupy the field.

Chapter 23
Effective Sentences

♦EXERCISE 23.A - ACTIVE AND PASSIVE VOICE

This exercise should be done after reading Section 23.1.1 in the *Handbook*.

♦After labeling the subject of the sentence with "S" and the verb with "V" and the direct object with "O" (if there is an object), decide whether each sentence below is active or passive voice.

1.   The plaintiff accepted the settlement offer.

2.   Texas law requires a balancing of circumstances presented in each individual case.

3.   This term will be arbitrarily defined by either a judge or jury.

4.   In the absence of legislative direction, the court has reluctantly followed this trend.

5.   The case for the defendant may be strengthened by considering the relative cost to the various parties.

6.   The prescriptive easement had been established by the objective acts of the claimant.

7.   The claimant's objective acts had established the prescriptive easement.

8.   The Whalers' right to use the access road can be revoked by Mrs. Townsend.

9.   Mrs. Townsend can revoke the Whalers' right to use the access road.

10.   Historically, interpretation of the rule has been left to the court's discretion.

✦EXERCISE 23.B - PASSIVE VOICE

This exercise should be done after reading Section 23.1.2 in the *Handbook.*

✦The following sentences are all written in passive voice. In some cases even the dependent clauses (see Chap. 10.1) are in passive voice. Note how awkward passive voice makes many of these sentences. Rewrite the sentences in active voice and underline the verbs in both the main clauses and the subordinate clauses.

1.   Pearson & Sons Lawn Service is owned by Clyde Pearson.

2.   After Mr. Lee's truck was found in the ditch by Officer O'Neill, an ambulance was called for by Officer O'Neill.

3.   The idea that to prevent the dumping of toxic waste was intended by the legislature was

focused on by the Montana court.

4. Although the marijuana was not found in the bedroom by the police, a film canister filled with cocaine was found by Officer Miller.

5. Important particularities are stipulated in the fourth amendment: the place to be searched and the things to be seized must be stated in the warrant.

6. Fremont's argument that his right to privacy was violated by the broad scope of the search is supported by the *Anderson* court's language.

7. Apparently, the business car had been driven by Tom on prior occasions, but specific permission to drive the business car was not given to him by his father on the day of the accident.

8. The question of whether a non-viable fetus is a minor child has not been ruled on by the courts; however, the rights of non-viable fetuses in other areas of the law are recognized by the courts.

9. The fair market value of the tractor should be recovered by the Wilsons because the recovery of the fair market value of property that has been destroyed is provided for by Washington tort law.

10. A private nuisance is defined by statutory law as "everything not included as a public nuisance."

✦EXERCISE 23.C - PASSIVE VOICE

The exercise should be done after reading Section 23.3.3 in the *Handbook.*

✦Read each of the following sentences and decide if the passive voice in the underlined section is used effectively or ineffectively. Write "E" for effective or "I" for ineffective, and then briefly explain why and, if necessary, in what context the passive voice is effective or ineffective.

1. A lawful business <u>will not be enjoined</u> without a clear showing that it is impossible or impractical to eliminate its offensive features.

2. In the past, Big Yard Toys Inc. would hire a subcontractor to install the equipment only if such arrangements <u>were requested</u> by the purchaser.

3. For the next ten years, the easement <u>was used</u> by all the landowners.

4. The plaintiff has testified that she <u>was assaulted</u> by a white male with blue eyes and blond hair. The defendant is a white male with brown eyes and black hair.

5. Testimony from the attending physician corroborates the victim's testimony that she <u>was struck</u> from behind.

6. Cathy's Creations is a designer clothing company <u>owned by</u> Cathy Nock. Ms. Nock employs a small staff to assist in the design and manufacture of the clothing.

7. Traditionally, if any element to a contract <u>has been omitted</u>, the contract is invalid.

8. Before the accidental poisoning, some of Mrs. Harris's medication <u>had been placed</u> in an old vitamin bottle.

9.   A standard form contract that detailed the terms of the agreement <u>was signed</u> by both

        parties.

10.   The Dead Man Statute <u>was intended</u> "to prevent the invasion of a deceased person's estate

        . . . ."

✦EXERCISE 23.D CONCRETE SUBJECTS

This exercise should be done after reading Section 23.2 in the *Handbook.*

✦Mark the subject and verb in the following sentences with an "S" and "V" and then revise the
sentence to have a concrete subject. In some cases, you will have to create your own concrete
subject.

1.   It could be argued by the defense that Mr. Smith was out of the state at the time of the

        robbery.

2.   It is clear that both parties intended to enter into a contract.

3.   It is highly unlikely that a fair market value existed for the poem.

4. Endorsement of the check is required before the funds can be transferred.

5. It would appear that our request for punitive damages will be granted.

6. Congressional confirmation is required for all federal judicial appointments.

7. It is a known fact that the defendant was refused admission to medical school because of his criminal record.

8. The aspect of the case that will be difficult to discount is Mr. Nolan's fingerprints on the knife.

9. It should be pointed out that South Land Timber's shipments to all three customers were consistently late.

10.   The factor of the defendant's earlier perjury conviction caused the jury to discount her

testimony in this case.

✦Exercise 23.E - Action Verbs

This exercise should be done after reading Section 23.3 in the *Handbook*.

✦Mark the subject and verb in the following sentences with an "S" and "V" and then revise the sentence to have a more effective action verb. In sentences beginning with *there* the subject will follow the verb.

1.   The way that a court determines mutual assent is to look at the objective manifestations

of the parties' actions.

2.   The governor made a statement that he would not testify for the defense.

3.   The jury had knowledge of the defendant's prior record.

4.   There are several facts that must be confirmed by that witness.

5. *Hanford v. Goehry* concerned a car that was kept at the father's place of business.

6. The nurse made an attempt to disconnect the life support system.

7. The *Harbeson* court made the suggestion that the Florida courts are moving towards awarding compensation for loss without applying the old standards.

8. There were no instances where the Parkers asserted their rights against the Lindquists.

9. *State v. Hughes* involved a defendant who shot two police officers while resisting arrest for another murder.

10. The two heirs are in disagreement over the division of property.

✦EXERCISE 23.F   SUBJECT-VERB DISTANCE

This exercise should be done after reading Section 23.4 in the *Handbook*.

✦Mark the subject and verb with "S" and "V" and then revise the sentence so that the subject and verb are closer together.

1. A standard form contract that detailed all the terms of the agreement except for the shipper's liability was signed by both parties.

2. Goods that sell for over five hundred dollars ($500.00) must have the transaction in writing.

3. The possibility that an intoxicated driver may decide to continue driving rather than be arrested after pulling over to the shoulder of the road is what influenced the legislature to revise the statute.

4. Another theory available to Mr. Henderson but not to his co-defendants is the "moral right doctrine."

5. Lloyd's statement to his tax preparer that "the lunches were really social" indicates that Lloyd intentionally misrepresented at least some of the information.

6. The court's reading of the written contract, despite its insistence that there was no accompanying oral agreement, favored the tire manufacturer.

7. The court in another case involving the revision of a law manual stated that "the purchase of a copyright did not carry with it a license to defame . . . ."

8. Our client's name and reputation as a upstanding citizen and honest businessman who treats his employees fairly have been injured by the libelous conduct of *Trade Union World*.

9. The concept of voluntary assumption of duty, when applied to the instant case, suggests that the State voluntarily assumed a duty to use due care in conducting inspections of nursing homes.

10.   The state's argument that it owes a duty only to the public generally and not to any

individual is not persuasive.

✦EXERCISE 23.G   SUBJECT-VERB REVIEW

This exercise should be done after reading Section 23.4 in the *Handbook*.

✦In the following excerpt from a client letter, the ineffective subject/verb units have been underlined. First, decide why the subject/verb unit is ineffective (ineffective use of passive voice, weak subject, weak verb, too much distance between subject and verb) and then revise for an effective subject/verb unit.

Dear Ms. Jones:

My research on your claim against your ex-landlord, Joe Printer, for the return of your
        1S
damage deposit is complete, and I think you will be pleased with the results. The basis for my
                1V   2S
opinion is current statutory provisions and the following facts you related during your visit to my
        2V
office.

On March 1, 1983, you entered into a valid written lease agreement. That lease was
                                                                                                    3S   3V
terminated effective May 5, 31, 1985, when you delivered a signed letter to Mr. Printer to that

effect.

This letter of notice of termination was received with at least 30 days' notice and was
            4S   4V   4V
accepted as valid. As of September 10, 1985 you are without reimbursement of your $200.00
                                                                            5S 5V
security deposit and you are without a written explanation from your former landlord telling why
                        5S 5V

78

he has not returned the money. Since the termination of your lease, four <u>letters</u> to Mr. Printer
6S
inquiring about the deposit <u>have been sent</u> by you. Although you left a forwarding address, you
6V
have not received a reply. The <u>apartment was left</u> clean and undamaged, except for normal wear
7S   7V
and a small crack in the bedroom window.

The issue is whether under these circumstances you can force Mr. Printer to refund your

$200.00 security deposit. An <u>examination</u> of the relevant Iowa statute currently in effect <u>reveals</u>
8S   8V
that you have a strong chance of recovering your deposit.

Generally, the <u>requirement</u> in the law for landlords <u>is</u> that within thirty days of termination
9S   9V
and receipt of the tenant's new address they must either return the damage deposit or provide the

tenant with a written statement listing reasons for withholding the deposit. Since no <u>refund</u> or
10S
<u>statement was sent</u> by Mr. Printer, the law seems to support your claim.
   10S   10V

✦EXERCISE 23.H   SENTENCE LENGTH

This exercise should be done after reading Section 23.5.1 in the *Handbook*.

✦For each of the following overly long sentences, revise either by breaking the sentence into two or more shorter sentences or by using punctuation to create manageable units of meaning within the sentence.

1.   Traditionally, Florida courts have deferred to the legislature's policy judgment on the

propriety of punitive damages awards and have manifested this deference by adhering

rigidly to the rule that punitive damages should be awarded with the greatest caution and

only where specifically authorized by statutes.

2.   The two critical factors the court will examine in determining whether a private citizen is an instrument or agent of the government are (1) the government's knowledge or acquiescence and (2) the intent of the party performing the search.

3.   Infringement is an interference with the rights granted to another under a law, a regulation, or a contract, and is usually categorized as infringement of copyrights, infringements of patents, or infringement of trademarks.

4.   In *Board of Regents*, the court held that a jury instruction regarding arson was correctly withheld from the jury by the trial court because the theory of arson was only a mere possibility and did not rise above speculation and conjecture.

5.   In *E.I. duPont de Nemorus & Co., Inc. v. Christopher*, the defendants used an airplane to photograph the plaintiff's Beaumont plant, which contained, in an open area, a secret but thus far unpatented process for producing methanol that had been developed by duPont at considerable time and expense and that provided duPont with a significant advantage over its competitors.

6.   The insurance adjuster's testimony that the defendant's brakes were not functioning properly was based upon a physical inspection of the accident area for skid marks both the night of the accident and the next day during daylight where he found one distinct skid mark and one virtually non-existent skid mark.

7.   Question Presented

Under a negligence *per se* or a common law theory of negligence, is a tavern

owner liable for serving alcohol to a minor without checking her identification

and continuing to serve alcohol to her after she spilled a drink and sang while on

top of a table, and later a personal injury car accident occurred when the car she

was driving collided with another vehicle?

8.   The plaintiff may obtain a summary of facts known and opinions held by the

nontestifying expert through depositions of occupants of the cars or through another

expert evaluating the facts and making his or her own conclusions.

9.   Question Presented

Under N.Y. Penal Law §125.25(3) (McKinney 1975), the felony murder rule,

would a charge of second degree murder be valid for a defendant who was one of

three participants in a robbery of a store owner with a previous heart condition

who subsequently died of a massive heart attack that his physician states was

undoubtedly caused by the stress of the robbery?

10.   The felony-murder rule applies regardless of the victim's previous heart condition and the

foreseeability of his death because robbery is inherently dangerous to human life and because a nexus has been established between the robbery and homicide.

✦**EXERCISE 23.1 SENTENCE LENGTH**

This exercise should be done after reading Section 23.5.1 in the *Handbook.*

✦Read the following excerpt from the beginning of a discussion section for an office memo. Most of the sentences are too long. Revise by (a) breaking up a sentence into two or more separate sentences, (b) using punctuation breaks to create a manageable unit of meaning within a sentence, and © eliminating unnecessary wordiness.

Discussion

In 1974, Congress voted on and then passed the Equal Credit Opportunity Act (hereinafter ECOA) in order to ensure that all financial institutions and all other firms engaged in or otherwise involved in the extension of credit make that credit equally available to all customers who are worthy of credit without regard to their sex or marital status. *Equal Credit Opportunity Act of Oct. 28, 1974*, Pub. L. No. 93-495, §502, 88 Stat. 1521 (1974) (current version at 15 U.S.C. §§1691-1691(f) (1982). In 1976, Congress expanded the ECOA to prohibit credit discrimination based on race, color, national origin, age, receipt of public assistance income, or the exercise in good faith of the rights guaranteed under the Consumer Credit Protection Act. *Equal Credit Opportunity Act Amendments of 1976*, Pub. L. No. 94-239, §§1-8, 90 Stat. 251 (1975) (current version at 15 U.S.C. §§1691-1691(f) (1982)).

The ECOA was enacted as a consumer protection statute designed to provide accurate information to and about customers involved in credit transactions and an antidiscrimination statute designed to shield protected classes of consumers from discrimination in the granting of credit. The Federal Reserve Board promulgated regulations to further those statutory goals. John H. Matheson, *The Equal Credit Opportunity Act: A Functional Failure*, 21 Harv. J. on Legis. 371 (1984).

✦EXERCISE 23.J   SENTENCES REVIEW

This exercise should be done after reading Section 23.5.3 in the *Handbook.*

✦Read the following excerpts from a memorandum of points and authorities in opposition to motion for temporary custody (your client is Mr. Barker). Decide (1) if any of the sentences are overly long, (2) if there is sufficient variety in the sentence lengths, and (3) if short sentences have been used effectively. Revise accordingly.

1.   Mr. Barker is a stable, loving father, who will provide a stimulating home environment for the Barkers' two children, George and Karen. However, the psychiatrist's report suggests that Mr. Barker may be compulsive. CP 37. This trait is not unusual for a highly successful businessman who now, because of that success, has more flexibility in his work schedule and will have even more time for his children. CP 41. Furthermore, the psychologist's report agrees that Mr. Barker has potential to be a sensitive, outgoing, yet stable parent.

2.   Mrs. Barker's psychological stability, however, is far from certain. She has been diagnosed as having histrionic tendencies and as being mildly hysterical. Mrs. Barker's psychologist states that these disorders make her prone to alcohol and chemical dependency. Once, this dependency became so severe that Mrs. Barker required medical

care to cope with her alcoholism.

3.   Mrs. Barker may contend that the court should apply the tender years doctrine, which

presumes that young children of "tender years" should be raised by the mother, and grant

her custody of the two children. The Barker children are not of tender years. In fact,

according to the psychologist's report, both George (age 17) and Karen (age 15) are

bright, articulate, and mature for their ages. CP 26.

✦EXERCISE 23.K   SENTENCES REVIEW

This exercise should be done after reading Section 23.5.3 in the *Handbook*.

✦Read the following fact statement from the plaintiff's memorandum of law and authorities.
Revise to improve sentence length by dividing overly long sentences, using short sentences for
emphasis, and eliminating wordiness.

Lester and Marie Franklin, plaintiffs, (Franklins) operate a combination grocery

store and delicatessen at 704 Filbert Street, San Francisco, California, on premises owned

by Tyler and Tina Morgan (Morgans).

On September 22, 1985, the Franklins and Morgans entered into a lease

agreement for the premises for eighteen (18) years with an option to terminate at the end

of the (10) years. (See lease agreement attached as Exhibit A.) In essence, the lease

provided for payment of base rent, percentage rent, taxes, and insurance and permitted the

Franklins to perform tenant improvements as approved by the Morgans.

Additionally, under the lease (Ex. A Paragraph 5) the Franklins agreed to maintain and repair the premises, except for the roof, exterior walls and foundation, which were reserved to the Morgans and made their responsibility.

While the Franklins were making the pre-approved tenant improvements, the City of San Francisco performed an inspection and determined that the brick parapets, which are part of the exterior wall existing above the roof line, needed to have seismic bracing work performed. Without this bracing, the City would not grant the final permit to allow Franklin to open their business.

It is important to point out that the seismic bracing was not part of the tenant improvements prepared by the Franklins and approved by the Morgans. Further, the seismic bracing was not required because of the character of the Franklins' business and would have been required for any tenant, regardless of the business being conducted on the premises.

At the time the requirement for seismic bracing arose and was made mandatory by the City of San Francisco, the Morgans were unavailable, vacationing in Mexico. Consequently, they were not available to perform the repairs, although the lease provisions specifically reserved to the Morgans the responsibility for the exterior walls. Faced with the proposition of being unable to open their business and thereby incurring substantial damages and possibly increased costs to perform the repairs, the Franklins chose to advance and pay for the cost of the repairs and then recoup the cost from the Morgans, pursuant to the lease terms.

The Franklins immediately paid the construction and engineering costs and sought reimbursement from the Morgans, who refused payment, contending that the Franklins accepted the premises "as is" and further, that although the bracing was required on a part of the structure specifically reserved to the Morgans, the bracing did not constitute a repair.

At the time of the arbitration, the case sits in this posture: The Franklins are seeking recovery from the Morgans for the amount to repair the exterior wall, and the Morgans are is seeking a judgment that they are not responsible for the repair cost.

✦EXERCISE 23.L EMPHASIS

This exercise should be done after reading Sections 23.6.1 - 23.6.4 in the *Handbook*.

✦Use the positions of emphasis and changes in punctuation to make the required revisions for emphasis.

Use sentence A for numbers 1 and 2:

> (A) The girl was tied to a tree and wearing only her shoes when the police officers found her.

1. Revise sentence A to emphasize that the girl was tied to a tree.

2. Revise sentence A to emphasize that the girl was wearing only shoes.

Use sentence B for number 3:

> (B) On July 14, 1986, a nuclear accident that killed seven people and that was the first fatal accident at the Nevada site occurred at Beatty, Nevada.

3.   Revise sentence B to emphasize that seven people were killed and that this was the first fatal accident at this site.

Use sentence C for number 4:

(C)   A judge has the option of sentencing him to a period of two to ten years and imposing a fine not to exceed $5,000 if the defendant is convicted of this offense.

4.   Revise sentence C to emphasize the possible jail term.

Use sentence D for number 5:

(D)   The plaintiff's final argument will depend on whether he can prove an over $20,000 depreciation of the value of his property.

5.   Revise sentence D to emphasize the $20,000.

Use sentence E for numbers 6 and 7:

(E)   Under the Uniform Building Code, the tenant has no maintenance obligations; the owner is obliged to maintain the building.

6.   Revise sentence E to emphasize that it is the owner has the maintenance responsibility.

7.   Revise sentence E to emphasize that the tenant is not obligated to maintain the building.

Use sentence F for number 8:

(F)   The fact that the dog has bitten three people is our proof that he is vicious.

8.   Revise sentence F to emphasize that the dog has bitten three people.

Use sentence G for numbers 9 and 10:

(G)   The church freely admits that it did not have a special use permit when it operated a full-time school.

9.   Revise sentence G to emphasize that the church had no special use permit.

10.   Revise sentence G to emphasize that the church makes the admission freely.

◆EXERCISE 23.M   SINGLE WORD EMPHASIZERS

This exercise should be done after reading Section 23.6.5 in the *Handbook*.

◆Using the suggested single word emphasizer, revise the following sentences. Some restructuring of the sentence may be necessary.

1.   Although five witnesses have placed Sharon Clark at the scene of the crime, she claims

       she was at home alone. (STILL)

2.   An explosives expert testified that a slight change in the cabin pressure would activate the

       detonator. (ANY)

3.   According to company regulations, an employee could not leave his or her post until the supervisor on duty had assigned a replacement. (NO)

4.   In the union's history, an allegation of this severity has not been made. (NEVER)

5.   It was the deceased who ran the stoplight. The defendant did not run the stoplight. (Revise into one sentence and use comma + NOT)

6.   The bonds in the safety deposit box were under her name. (ALL)

7.   The bonds in the safety deposit box were under her name. (ONLY)

8.   The members of the union voted to ratify the contract. (EVERY)

9.   Despite numerous warnings from the Environmental Protection Agency, National Chemical disposed of waste by-products by dumping them into the bay. (STILL)

10. The operation did not cause Laura Smith's death. She died from inadequate post-operative care. (Revise into one sentence and use comma + NOT.)

✦EXERCISE 23.N   CHANGING WORD ORDER

This exercise should be done after reading Section 23.6.6. in the *Handbook*.

✦Change the normal word order in the following sentences to emphasize the part that is underlined.

1. The defendant was later identified <u>in a lineup with no other bearded men</u>.

2. The defendant forced Ms. Harper to perform fellatio <u>at gunpoint</u>.

3. Two witnesses have identified <u>the starter's pistol</u> as the weapon used.

4. The trial court's exercise of this discretion will be overturned on appeal <u>only for a manifest abuse</u>.

5. Mere assertions do not satisfy <u>the burden of proof</u>.

6. The defendant could have effectively corrected all alleged errors <u>at the time they were made</u>.

7. The State had strong evidence <u>on each separate count</u>.

8. The definition of deadly weapon includes <u>the words "pistol"</u> <u>and "revolver."</u>

9. The defendant's motion to sever Counts I and II from Counts III, IV, and V was <u>also denied</u>.

10. The defendant was convicted by the jury <u>on all five counts</u>.

✦EXERCISE 23.0   BREAKING A PATTERN

This exercise should be done after reading Section 23.6.8 in the *Handbook*.

✦From each group of sentences, formulate one sentence or a sequence of sentences that uses a pattern. When appropriate, deliberately break the pattern for emphasis.

1. There is a clear pattern in Mr. Baylor's behavior. He started by intimidating his children.

   His next victim of intimidation was his wife. Now he has been intimidating a witness.

2. In October, Thomas Dever threatened Miss Stein. At the time he was not insane. He was

   also not insane when he shadowed her for two weeks in November and when, on

   Christmas Eve, he brutally killed her.

3. We want to believe that our country acted fairly and wisely. It is hard for us to believe that it acted maliciously.

4. After twenty years in prison, Carl Wilson returned to society. He didn't have a job or a home. He had no money in the bank.

5. The opposition lacks proof that the defendant was at the scene of the crime. Furthermore, they cannot prove that he had a motive, much less that he committed the deed.

6. Neither a court nor a jury can undo what Frank Morris has done. Even a jail term will not undo what he has done.

7. Desmond Adams rebuilt his business with his own money. He did all the hard work, and he did not depend upon the help of his former partners.

8. Judith Davis, not her husband Martin, refused to see a marriage counselor. She was also the one who filed for divorce. Now she wants an even larger share of his pension.

9.   Kyle Davis had a silent partner, Ronald Thomas, in the contract for the Lowell building

       and in the contract for the Madison complex. He acted alone in the contract for the

       Westside shopping mall.

10.   With malice aforethought, Michael Mann bought a .38 caliber pistol at Seaside Pawn

       Shop and then waited in his car for Howard Peterson to return home from work and then

       followed him up to his front door and shot him three times in the chest.

✦EXERCISE 23.P EMPHASIS APPLICATION

This exercise should be done after reading Section 23.6 in the *Handbook*.

✦Using a memo or brief that you have already written, check to see if you have used either of the two weaker strategies for emphasis: (1) telling the reader what is important or (2) underlining. Also check to see if you have used <u>clearly</u>, <u>obviously</u>, or <u>very</u> as single word emphasizers. Where appropriate, revise by omitting these strategies for emphasis or using another strategy for emphasis.

✦EXERCISE 23.Q EMPHASIS APPLICATION

This exercise should be done after reading Section 23.6 in the *Handbook*.

◆Using a memo or brief that you have already written, check for the following strategies for emphasis. Revise where appropriate.

    a.   short sentences
    b.   positions of emphasis
    c.   punctuation for emphasis
    d.   single word emphasizers
    e.   changes in normal word order
    f.   repetition of key words
    g.   patterns

Chapter 24
Effective Words

◆EXERCISE 24.A - WORD CHOICE

This exercise should be done after reading Sections 24.1.1 - 24.1.3 in the *Handbook*.

◆Find the inappropriate or imprecise word choice(s) in each of the following sentences. Write in the word(s) that you think expresses (express) the writer's intended meaning.

1. All of these factors exhibit that it would be in the best interest for the children to modify the child custody agreement.

2. The court will constitute this as an established custodial environment.

3. This memorandum will display how this statute applies to Ms. Lynch's claim.

4. The court may have psychological tests given to the kids.

5. The *Gertz* court explored to find if Gertz had availed himself to the press.

6. It is tough to know whether the court would award a partial injunction against the health club.

7.	Washington State courts have adopted the general and the limited public figure tests

	annunciated in *Gertz.*

8.	The corporation ceased in August 1982.

9.	The trial court decreed that the plaintiffs should be awarded damages and decreed a

	permanent injunction against keeping swine in excess of one boar, two brood sows, and

	their litters not over six months old.

10.	The commission was set to oversee health care.

11.	All these things must be proved beyond a preponderance of the evidence.

12.	In *Yee v. Dept. of Environmental Services, Multnomah County*, 826 F.2d 877, 881 (1987),

	the court found that an American of Chinese dissent is a member of a class of persons

	protected on the basis of race.

13.	When Duckworth tied the handkerchief around McCormack's jaw, he exasperated her

	condition by inhibiting her flow of oxygen.

14.	Under the Federal Tort Claims Act, which evokes Washington law of respondeat

	superior, is the government liable for the negligent act of its employee when that employee, while traveling from a temporary base in California to his home base in Washington and while traveling in a rented car supplied by the government, subsequently hit a civilian's car when reentering the highway after he took a lunch break and a short sightseeing trip and caused extensive personal injuries to the civilian?

✦EXERCISE 24.B CONSISTENT TERMS

This exercise should be done after reading Section 24.1.4 in the *Handbook*.

✦Revise the following excerpt from a memo so that the writer uses the same term for the same idea.

A court will need to examine the tests for two doctrines, *respondeat superior* and "loaned servant," to determine whether Dr. Robinson or Bondurant Temporary Agency, Inc. (Bondurant) can be held vicariously liable for the complete destruction of Ms. Bakerman's coat. The first doctrine, *respondeat superior*, has a three-prong test. The first two prongs of the test are met. First, Carol Kester was negligent for the destruction of the coat. *See Nyman v. MacRae Bros. Constr. Co.*, 69 Wash. 2d 285, 287, 418 P.2d 253, 254 (1966). Second, Carol was acting within the scope of her employment at the time of the tortious act. *See Kuehn v. White*, 24 Wash. App. 274, 277, 600 P.2d 679, 682 (1979). There will, however, be a dispute about the third test: whether Carol was under the control of Bondurant, her general employer, or under the control of Dr. Robinson, her temporary employer at the time the coat was destroyed. *See Kroshus v. Koury*, 30 Wash. App. 258, 263, 633 P.2d 909, 911 (1981) (quoting *McLean v. St. Regis Paper Co.*, 6 Wash. App. 727, 732, 496 P.2d 571, 574 (1972)).

The second defense, "loaned servant," has a three-part test to determine who has control of a temporary employee. *Pichler v. Pacific Mechanical Constr.*, 1 Wash App. 447, 450-51, 462 P.2d 960, 963 (1969). The first and second parts of the test--who has the right to select or hire and fire the servant and who has the right to direct how the servant shall perform his duties--will be disputed, but the most important test will be who had exclusive control or the right to exclusive control at the time of the tortious act. *Pichler*, 1 Wash. App. at 450-51, 462 P.2d at 963.

✦ EXERCISE 24.C - APPROPRIATE COMPARISONS

This exercise should be done after reading Section 24.1.6 in the *Handbook*.

✦ Revise the following sentences and paragraphs so that the same term is used for the same idea and so that appropriate comparisons are being made (for example, comparing a case to another case is an appropriate comparison, comparing a defendant to a case is not.) If the sentence is already correct, simply mark it as correct.

1.   The grief over the loss of a six-week-old fetus is hardly comparable to a viable fetus.

2.   This policy of protecting the investor from the various schemes devised by promoters has been a persuasive cornerstone for judicial interpretation of investment contracts in the post-*Howey* era. *See, e.g., SEC v. Glenn W. Turner Enter., Inc.*, 474 F.2d 476 (9th Cir. 1973). However, the Ninth Circuit apparently does not find consumer protection alone determinative when interpreting federal securities law. Other factors may come into play, such as the underlying nature of the financial relationship between the buyer and the

promoter. *See, e.g., Brodt v. Bache & Co., Inc.,* 595 F.2d 459 (9th Cir. 1978). Consequently, legal analysis of CP's money-making scheme does not yield a precise conclusion about whether a Ninth Circuit federal court would deem it to be an investment contract.

3. The problem with comparing *Turner* to the instant case is that the court offers no explanation about why the common enterprise prong was satisfied.

4. A potential plaintiff would argue that the fetus is the personal property of the mother. This argument would be similar to *Moore* in that the body part that was surgically removed was the personal property of the plaintiff patient.

5. In its decision, the *Brodt* court explicitly rejected using the concept of "horizontal commonality" employed in other circuits; that approach would require that there be a pooling of interests combined with a pro-rata sharing of profits. *Id.* at 460. Instead, the court used the broader principle of "vertical commonality," which requires that the investor and the promoter be involved in some common venture without mandating that other investors also be involved in the venture. *Id.* at 461 (citing *Hector v. Wiens,* 533 F.2d 429 (9th Cir. 1976)).

✦EXERCISE 24.D - SUBJECT-VERB-OBJECT COMBINATIONS

This exercise should be done after reading Section 24.1.6 in the *Handbook*.

✦Isolate the subject, verb, and object and read them together to determine whether the subject/verb/object combinations in the following sentences make sense. When necessary, revise for precision. (The subject/verb/object mismatch may be in the main clause or in a subordinate clause.)

1.   The language of the courts since then has broadened.

2.   As for the burden of proof, *Eggert* says that the burden is on the plaintiff to establish a right to maintain the action in an action for conversion.

3.   Should Mr. Robinson bring suit, the great weight of the case law would deny him relief.

4.   A conviction under section 1071 in the Fourth Circuit has been interpreted as requiring proof of four elements: 1) that a federal warrant had been issued for the fugitive's arrest; 2) that the defendant had knowledge that a warrant had been issued for the fugitive's arrest; 3) that the defendant actually harbored or concealed the fugitive; and 4) that the defendant intended to prevent the fugitive's discovery or arrest.

5.   There are, however, public policy issues that argue persuasively to restrict a woman's

        right to fetal tissue.

6.   The test for whether a nuisance exists is determined by the use to which the property is

        put.

7.   The likelihood that the court will determine that this is an established custodial

        environment is favorable.

8.   The trust fund doctrine, which was created by the equity courts to protect creditors when

        an indebted corporation dissolved, withheld the corporation's property to be used to pay

        off debts.

9.   Even though New Age aerobics may not be causing safety hazards, increased traffic

        congestion, or unsightly buildings, the cumulative effects of its activities should be

        considered.

10. The probability that Mrs. Davis can meet this required standard of proof is unlikely.

✦EXERCISE 24.E - GRAMMATICAL AMBIGUITIES

This exercise should be done after reading Section 24.1.7 in the *Handbook*.

✦Do exercises 26.L, 26.M, 26.N, and 26.O of the *Practice Book* on dangling and misplaced modifiers.

✦EXERCISE 24.F - CONCISENESS

This exercise should be done after reading Sections 24.2.1 - 24.2.5 in the *Handbook*.

✦Revise the following sentences for wordiness by creating strong subject-verb units and by editing out expletives and throat clearing expressions.

1. There are two defenses available to Acme.

2. It seems more likely than not that you are bound by the written agreement simply because you signed it.

3. In determining whether there was a sudden emergency, courts also take into consideration whether there was sufficient warning that should have alerted the driver to the imminent danger.

4.   The court will give Fed. R. Civ. P. 4(d)(1) a liberal construction.

5.   A court might have the inclination to follow the view that "in a highly mobile and affluent society, it is unrealistic to interpret 4(d)(1) so that the person to be served has only one dwelling house or usual place of abode at which process may be left." 4A Charles Alan Wright & Arthur R. Miller, *Federal Practice and Procedures* §1096, (2d ed. 1987).

6.   There is a difference in opinion between the two parties over whether the deposit is refundable.

7.   The court used the inference that because the papers were left with appellant's mother, the appellant received them.

8.   It appears that if "substantial" is held to be analogous with "principal," then five percent of a total business would be the minimum necessary to establish that certain sales of merchandise are a "principal" part of a business.

9. An argument could be made that Ms. Fox so conditioned her acceptance of your offer as to create a counteroffer.

10. It was the legislature's intention to encourage corporations to explore new ways of reducing energy costs.

11. After thoroughly researching your complaint against Mr. Brown, I have come to the conclusion that the best way to recover the $2,500 that he owes you is to file a lien against his orchard.

12. An important consideration to be kept in mind, however, is that the boys deny making any threats.

13. The defendant has made a motion to suppress the evidence seized after the arrest.

14. It was not error for the trial court to fail to instruct on the absence of intervening cause.

This exercise should be done after reading Sections 24.2.6 - 24.2.8 in the *Handbook*.

✦Revise and edit the following sentences for pompous language, doubling phrases, needless repetition, and clutter.

1. Before I can begin advising you about the various aspects of your case, I need to ask the following question about whether or not your husband knew or was aware that his life expectancy was very short.

2. Furthermore, in addition to the procedure that is utilized to initiate the process, the foreman of the plant must initiate the contingency or back-up system at that same point in time.

3. It is the night watchman's usual custom to terminate his rounds at 5 a.m. in the morning after carefully performing an inspection of each and every safe in the building.

4. Obviously, prior to trial, the defendant will move by filing a Motion in Limine to exclude all of the evidence of his previous prior convictions.

5. The nature of the consensus of opinion among board members was that to implement a certain procedure that would be used by each and every employee when entering or leaving the building would not terminate the problems and difficulties the company was experiencing from employee theft.

6. It was believed and assumed by the Parkers that in situations where real estate agents list a home for sale, the real estate agents have an obligation and responsibility to appraise and determine the value of the home that is being listed.

7. For a period of two months during the year of 1985, Mr. Wilson aided and abetted a known felon by allowing her to utilize his cabin as a place to hide from law enforcement officers who were looking for her.

8. At the present time, there is clearly no constitutionally protected right to receive credit, but however there is a great deal that can be done to guarantee and insure that credit is available to all people on a just and fair basis.

9.   In my own personal opinion, we cannot get an injunction from a court that will

       completely eliminate the use of the factory's noon whistle at 12:00 each day.

10.   Our principal and basic policy objective in promulgating the order to vacate the premises

       of the building was to insure and otherwise guarantee that all of the inhabitants and

       residents of said premises were safe and secure.

✦EXERCISE 24.H - CONCISENESS

This exercise should be done after reading Section 24.2.9 in the *Handbook*.

✦Edit the following sentences by reducing sentences to clauses, clauses to phrases, and phrases to words.

1.   In late October 1987, Kyle Nelson asked Frances Miles to house sit for him while he was

       away on vacation. Frances Miles is an acquaintance of Kyle Nelson.

2.   The trial judge calculated O'Hara's offender score as seven. She based her decision on

       Or. Rev. Stat. 137.370 (4). That statute states in part that "[u]nless the court expressly

       orders otherwise, a term of imprisonment shall be concurrent with the remainder of any

       sentence previously imposed at the time the court imposes sentence."

3.   Instruction 10 did not shift the ultimate burden of proof to Chin. Instruction 10 did not create any mandatory presumption. It did not impose any burden of producing evidence on Chin. Rather, the instruction states that the presumption "is not binding" upon the jury. It further states that the jury can determine "what weight, if any," to give to the presumption.

4.   At the disposition hearing, the state presented a document describing Ortega's prior criminal history. Ortega's prior criminal history consisted of ten burglary convictions and three minor offenses subject to diversion.

5.   Peters moved to Chesterville to be near her husband. Her husband was an inmate at the state penitentiary at Chesterville. Upon arriving in Chesterville, Peters met a woman. The woman's husband was also an inmate in the penitentiary.

6.   The legislature directed the Department of Ecology to publish a statutorily prescribed notice by four different means. These four different means are as follows: 1) publication of the notice once a year for five years in major as well as local newspapers; 2) publication of the notice every six months on radio and television stations broadcasting in every county; and 3) posting the notice in a conspicuous location in every county; and 4)

including a copy of the notice with notices of taxes due for 1972 mailed by each county treasurer.

7. The Court of Appeals upheld the rape conviction and corresponding habitual criminal finding. However, the Court of Appeals reversed the assault conviction.

8. At 2:20 a.m. on September 29, 1986, Brian Smith entered his parents' bedroom. His parents were sleeping there at the time. Brian shot his mother in the head with a 30.06 rifle. This shot killed his mother. Mr. Smith woke up. He saw Brian leave the bedroom. He was unable to telephone for help because Brian had taken the telephone off the hook in the kitchen. Mr. Smith locked the bedroom door. He escaped through the window. Brian returned to the bedroom. He intended to kill his father. He found that his father had escaped.

9. After the police arrived at the scene, the officers discovered Barbara Wilson-Hughes in a comatose condition. They immediately called an emergency medical unit. The emergency medical unit transported Mrs. Wilson-Hughes to a local hospital. At the hospital, she was treated for a "closed-head injury" and several facial lacerations.

10. In *Workman*, the court set forth and applied a two-prong test for restricting and otherwise

determining when lesser offense instructions should be given to the jury to use in its

deliberations. The first prong of the test is that each of the elements of the lesser offense

must be a necessary element of the offense charged. The second prong of the test is that

evidence must support an inference that the lesser crime was committed.

✦EXERCISE 24.I - CONCISENESS REVIEW

This exercise should be done after reading Section 24.2 in the *Handbook*.

✦Using all the strategies for concise writing in this section, revise and edit the following
sentences for wordiness.

1. Damages in the amount of $20,000 were paid to each plaintiff.

2. Clearly, a driver of a motor vehicle who basically refuses to wear the glasses prescribed

for him by his doctor and who continues to operate his vehicle at a rate of speed that

exceeds the speed limit is an extremely dangerous hazard on the road.

3. Testimony was elicited from Trooper Evans. Trooper Evans investigated the accident.

Trooper Evans testified that the "primary casual factor" of the accident had been the

defendant's intoxicated state.

4. Apparently, there are two arguments Jones will make in his own defense. Jones will first make the argument that, prior to the search, he did not knowingly, willingly, and voluntarily give Officer Smith his consent to a search of his wallet. Jones will then make a second argument that the items that Smith discovered during the course of the search, most particularly the stolen charge card, exceeded and otherwise went beyond the scope of the consent that Jones gave to Officer Smith.

5. Henson responded to the public disclosure request by providing all of the documents, except two letters. These two letters were excluded because of the fact that both of these letters contained proprietary or private information with regard to the business practices of Henson.

6. For the most part, each of their mail was sent to each of their separate addresses, but sometimes, on occasion, an invitation would come to the address of Mr. Jones, and both of their names would be present on the invitation.

7. Basically, Mr. McRae stated in a formal statement that he discussed only the manufacture and delivery of the equipment with Jim Drane. Jim Drane is the principal of Lakeland

Elementary. Mr. McRae reiterated over again that they did not discuss the matter of installation.

8.   Based on a recognition of the fact that in cases very similar to yours in their facts the courts invariably issued a directed verdict, I am of the opinion that we can, with all probability, hope for and expect that you too will be granted a directed verdict in your case.

9.   For all intents and purposes, the court was absolutely correct when it issued a denial of defendant's motion for a new trial for the very specific reason that the defendant must do more than merely suggest a "possibility of prejudice" when he moves for a new trial.

10.   Due to the fact that my client was absolutely unaware of and uninformed about the state and federal law governing this matter and due to her advanced age and years, she should be considered for and granted special consideration by this court. Her primary and only desire was and is to give and bequeath her most prized and valuable collection of hand-painted china to the library of the community in which she has lived and resided during these past eighty-seven years.

112

This exercise should be done after reading Section 24.2 in the *Handbook*.

✦Revise and edit the following paragraphs for wordiness.

1. As established in *Park v. Stolzheise*, 24 Wash. 2d 781, 167 P.2d 412 (1946), "comfortable enjoyment means both mental quiet and physical comfort." With regard to this definition, the neighbors will obviously argue that the floodlights being on until 12 midnight adversely affects their physical comfort in that their sleep is greatly disturbed by the bright lights beaming through the bedroom windows of the houses. To support this contention, the neighbors will further argue the *Bruskland* case where the court stated that headlights of an automobile that shined upon a bedroom window of a dwelling house unreasonably and substantially interfered with the comfort and enjoyment of the owners' property, thus constituting a private nuisance. 42 Wash. 2d at 348. Consequently, therefore, it can be stated that the trial court or trial judge or jury would probably rule that the comfortable enjoyment of the neighbors of their property was interfered with by the shining of the floodlights.

2. Besides determining whether there was a pre-existing controversy , the court must also determine whether the plaintiff "thrust into the controversy in an attempt to influence the outcome." *Hutchinson*, 443 U.S. at 135. An example of thrusting into a controversy in an attempt to influence the outcome of the issues is found in *Waldbaum*. In *Waldbaum*, a controversy was developing in the supermarket industry. People were debating about the

113

introduction of unit pricing and open dating into supermarkets. The plaintiff in *Waldbaum* purposefully attempted to influence the outcome of this public debate by holding a special meeting to which it invited both the press and the public.

3.   Although the two levels of immunity have been basically well defined, the level of immunity that parole board members should be afforded remains unclear and uncertain. In order to effectively analyze the case at hand, the court must assess the rules and tests of the jurisdictions governing this case. The court must examine the decisions of the Supreme Court, Third Circuit, and Ninth Circuit in regard to the levels of immunity accorded to public officials which will present the basic tests to determine the type and scope of immunity that the Board members should be afforded.

✦EXERCISE 24.K - LEGALESE

This exercise should be done after reading Section 24.3 in the *Handbook*.

✦Read the following opinion letter and eliminate the legalese.

Dear Mr. Patterson:

Enclosed herewithin is a copy of the Notice of Appeal that was filed with the King County Superior Court on November 25. Said notice will be transferred to the Court of Appeals forthwith.

Because the case involves an issue of constitutional magnitude, it will be reviewed de novo. Nonetheless, prevailing on appeal is unlikely and improbable. As previously discussed, show-ups are not per se impermissible. Hence of the Court of Appeals will need, iter alia, to balance suggestiveness against the reliability of the identifications. To wit, appellate court will consider the five factors seriatum and probably reach the same conclusion as previously reached by trial court.

In spite of the fact that these cases are infrequently and rarely reversed on appeal, the utmost effort and diligence will be exercised on your behalf by all those in our firm. If all else fails, a writ of certiori will be filed with the Supreme Court on your behalf if you so request.

Very truly yours,

Ms. Sarah Fisher

✦EXERCISE 24.L - GENDER-NEUTRAL LANGUAGE

This exercise should be done after reading Section 24.4 in the *Handbook*.

✦Substitute gender neutral language for the following phrases and sentences.

1. masked gunman

2. neighbor's wife (both husband and wife live together)

3. the family of man

4.   Dear Board of Governors and Governesses

5.   the woman driver in the second vehicle

✦EXERCISE 24.M - GENDER-NEUTRAL LANGUAGE

This exercise should be done after reading Section 24.4 in the *Handbook*.

✦Revise the following sentences by substituting gender neutral language for sexist language.

1.   The operator of the vehicle left the scene without identifying himself.

2.   When determining the status of a child as Indian, the state court must seek verification of his status from either the Bureau of Indian Affairs or from his tribe.

3.   Evidence of the defendant's other offenses may not be admitted as proof of the charged offense if the evidence is relevant only to show his criminal disposition.

4.   A guardian is a man lawfully invested with the power, and charged with the duty, of taking care of another who, for defect of age, understanding, or self-control, is considered unable to administer his own affairs.

5. Summary judgment should be denied if the moving party does not sustain his initial burden of proof and if reasonable men would reach different conclusions from the evidence presented.

6. When requesting that a judgment be set aside, the moving party's attorney must comply with CR 60(e)(1), which requires that he prepare an affidavit setting forth the facts constituting a defense.

7. The statute gives men and their wives more freedom to independently dispose of their property by contract, free from court supervision.

8. Mrs. Edwards is a working mother who has little time or energy left for her children at the end of the day. Mr. Edwards, on the other hand, operates his accounting business out of his home. Consequently, he is able to give the children the mothering they need.

9. The Acme Loan Service informed Mr. Valdez and his wife that the liens would have to be removed before they could secure a loan.

10. "It is the purpose of this subchapter to assure a meaningful disclosure of credit terms so that the consumer will be able to compare more readily the various credit terms available to him and avoid the uninformed use of credit, and to protect the consumer against inaccurate and unfair credit billing and credit card practices." 15 U.S.C. §1601 (a).

11. Rule 9 of the Admission to Practice Rules provides that a qualified law student, law clerk, or law school graduate may be granted a limited license to practice law if he 1) has completed at least two-thirds of a three-year course of studies, 2) has the written approval of his law school dean, and 3) has certified that he has read and is familiar with the Rules of Professional Conduct.

12. Miss Helene Russell was a lady pharmacist in Baton Rouge, Louisiana, when a federal grand jury indicted her on fifteen counts of violating Title 21 U.S.C. §§841(a)(1), 841(b)(2), 843(a)(4), and 827(a)(3).

13. The comment to subsection (a) of §158 explains that a man may invade another man's property by "throwing, propelling, or placing a thing" either on the land or in the air above it.

14. The airline's spokesman claimed that no man could have prevented the tragedy and that the accident was "an act of God."

15. The court may impose an exceptional sentence for the offense of indecent liberties when the victim is particularly vulnerable or unable to resist because of her young age and when the offender shows that he is not amenable to treatment.

✦EXERCISE 24.N GENDER-NEUTRAL LANGUAGE

This exercise should be done after reading Section 24.4 in the *Handbook*.

✦Revise the following paragraph for sexist language.

1. The incident giving rise to the attempted rape charge occurred on November 1, 1988, when the defendant, Harold Strickland, went out on a date with Connie Osburn. About 12:30 a.m., Strickland drove Connie back to his apartment. Once inside, Strickland immediately forced Connie into the bedroom and onto the bed. Without her consent, he lay on top of her and tried to force his hand under her clothing. Connie then convinced Strickland that she needed to use the bathroom. He relented and, while she was in the bathroom, Connie escaped through a window. After finding a policewoman, Connie took her to the scene and showed her Strickland's apartment.

✦**EXERCISE 26.A - FRAGMENTS**

This exercise should be done after reading Section 26.2 in the *Handbook.*

✦Read the following and decide if they are complete sentences or fragments. If they are fragments, revise to make complete sentences.

1.   The defendant's story will not be told. If the court allows the prior convictions to be

admitted into evidence.

2.   Mr. Barnett won a Pulitzer prize. Which generally gives a person worldwide recognition

for his or her work.

3.   When an artist and author like Michael Barnett creates a prize-winning musical, he has

two interests in the end product. The first interest is an economic one.

4.   The second interest, honor and reputation. "[T]he author wants to ensure that his creative

personality, expressed in his work, is preserved." Robert E. Hathaway II, *American Law*

Analogues to the Paternity Element of the Doctrine of Moral Right: Is the Creative Artist in America Really Protected? 30 Copyright L. Symp. 121, 122 (1976).

5. Both of these crimes are considered violent crimes. Therefore, probably not of probative value to the state's case.

6. Although a technical case can be made for non-compliance with Rule 4(d)(1), the question of the overall efficiency of this approach is open to doubt. Especially in the light of potential service in New York under the California long arm statute.

7. The trend in American courts to balance economic and moral interests in the areas of contract and tort law. In European countries, the opposite is true.

8. The court has only one real issue to decide. Whether the Los Angeles home is the dwelling house of the defendant.

9.   Unfair competition, a general term, embracing the narrower area of trademark law, which

concerns the same legal wrong, namely, misrepresentations as to the source of goods or

services.

10.   The defendant states that Ms. Patten gave the coins to him as a gift. Whereas Ms. Patten

alleges that she was robbed.

✦EXERCISE 26.B - FRAGMENTS

This exercise should be done after reading Section 26.2 in the *Handbook*.

✦Read the following statement of facts from an office memo. Find and revise all sentence
fragments.

Agnes and Arthur Hoffelmeir were on vacation between October 11 and October

20, 1985. Their neighbors, the Burgesses, offered to take care of their pet cat. Which the

Hoffelmeirs were emotionally attached to and considered a member of the family.

On October 19, 1985, the cat went into Mrs. Kravitz's rose garden and began

chewing the rose bushes. Although Mrs. Kravitz tried to shoo the cat away. The cat kept

returning to the Kravitz yard to chew on the rose bushes. Because this had happened on

several other occasions, Mrs. Kravitz called the Humane Society.

The Humane Society impounded the cat, and Mr. Janske of the Society tried

unsuccessfully to contact the Hoffelmeirs. The cat was destroyed on October 20, 1985.

Within 36 hours after impoundment and despite a city ordinance that states that an impounded dog must be held for at least 72 hours before it can be destroyed.

✦EXERCISE 26.C - FRAGMENTS REVIEW

This exercise should be done after reading Section 26.2 in the *Handbook*.

✦Read the following excerpt from the same memo about the destruction of a pet cat. Find and revise all fragments that are not permissible uses.

In *Sequin*, a federal customs official impounded the plaintiff's car and failed to release her car in a timely manner. The court held that if the defendant's conduct could be interpreted as willful or malicious, the plaintiff could recover damages for emotional distress. *Id.* at 811.

We could argue that the Humane Society and Mr. Janske acted unlawfully. If they both were bound by the Sequin City Ordinance. And because the cat was destroyed before the time provided by the ordinance.

The Humane Society and Mr. Janske may make the following arguments. First, that *Sequin* refers to the unlawful garnishment or seizure of property, not the destruction of it. Second, that they acted within their legal duty when the cat was seized. Third, because they did not intentionally violate the city ordinance, their actions were not willful or malicious. Also because Mr. Janske attempted to contact the Hoffelmeirs before the cat was destroyed.

The Hoffelmeirs could counter these claims with the following arguments. First,

124

the seizure of the cat may have been lawful. The destruction was not. While *Sequin* is concerned with the unlawful seizure of property, the unlawful destruction of property is even more serious. Therefore, the principle of *Sequin* should apply in this case.

Second, the destruction of the cat before the proscribed time period is malicious and willful misconduct. The Society and Mr. Janske being aware that pets are valuable to their owners. Mr. Janske should have waited until the Hoffelmeirs were contacted before the cat was destroyed. The city ordinance's requirement for a holding period so that pet owners will have an opportunity to claim their pets. If the Humane Society had abided by the ordinance, the cat would have been claimed, and the Hoffelmeirs would not have suffered this loss.

Third, given that the rationale against awarding punitive damages is that an injured party will be adequately compensated through other measures. And given that the replacement cost of the cat is not adequate compensation. The only way the Hoffelmeirs will receive adequate compensation is through an award of damages that includes compensation for mental anguish.

Finally, that there is persuasive authority to support the Hoffelmeirs' argument for damages for mental anguish. In a Louisiana case, a neighbor trapped the plaintiff's pet cat and brought it to the animal control center where the cat was destroyed. The plaintiffs sued to recover damages for the mental anguish and humiliation they suffered from the loss of their cat. The court held that they could be compensated for their mental anguish. If the plaintiffs suffered actual damages. *Peloquin v. Calcasier Parish Police Jury*, 367 So.2d 1246, 1251 (La. App. 1979).

✦EXERCISE 26.D - VERB TENSE

This exercise should be done after reading Section 26.3.1 in the *Handbook.*

✦Read the following sentences and, where necessary, correct the tense of the verbs.

1. The issue in *Farny* is whether the New Jersey address is the defendant's dwelling house or usual place of abode.

2. In *Farny*, the plaintiff contends that the New Jersey address continues to be defendant's dwelling house or usual place of abode.

3. Under Article III of the Constitution, the jurisdiction of federal courts is limited to cases and controversies. U.S. Const. art. III, §1.

4. In *Wagner*, the court held that the showup procedure was permissible, even though the police had asked the witness to identify a handcuffed suspect.

5. In *Kraus*, the court held that the show up was not impermissibly suggestive when the victim of an attempted robbery was asked to identify the suspect after the police brought

the suspect to the victim's place of business and when the police conducted a pat-down search of the suspect in front of the victim.

6.   Cases in the entertainment industry usually involve a misappropriation or attribution of one's name for economic gain.

7.   In *Bishop*, the court analyzed the predecessor to the current assault statute and concluded that aiming or discharging a firearm was not a lesser included offense of second degree assault.

8.   The State's evidence reveals that Michael informed the group that he had beaten McIvar.

9.   This court held that the *Edwards* construction must be read into the court rule as if that construction had been originally written into the rule.

10. Officer Thompson arrived at the scene of an accident in which a car towing a small trailer went over an embankment.

This exercise should be done after reading Section 26.3.1 in the *Handbook*.

♦Read the following paragraph and, where necessary, correct the tense of the verbs.

In 1956, Bob Rhumb built the Cummings's house. In May 1957, Rhumb builds a garage and fence, and John Miller buys the lot north of Rhumb's lot--the lot that is now Walker's--and builds a house on it that was completed toward the end of 1957.

When Rhumb finished building his garage and fence, he had planted his lawn, which extends along a line from the fence to the street. Rhumb did not plant the three-foot strip that is now in dispute.

In the spring of 1958, Miller plants that strip with grass after Rhumb agreed to pay for a portion of the costs. In addition, along the back portion of his property, Miller plants a garden that extends onto the three-foot strip.

From the time that Miller planted the lawn and garden in 1958 up to the present, he and the subsequent owners maintain the garden and mow the grass on the strip that is now in dispute.

During the time that he had owned the property, Rhumb never discusses the true boundary line with anyone, except for references to it on two occasions: once, in 1958, when he agreed with Miller to pay a portion of the grass seed costs, and again in 1973, during Kaiser's ownership, when Kaiser was out washing his car, he said something to Rhumb like "Hey, you oughta come over and wash my car 'cause I always mow your lawn."

In January 1978, the Kaisers sold the property to the Hemstads. The Hemstads live there until 1982 and then rent the house from 1982 until 1985, when they sell it to Debbie Walker. Walker and her predecessors have all maintained the garden and mowed the lawn just as the Millers did.

In 1989, our client, Charlie Cummings and his wife Anna buy the house previously occupied by Bob Rhumb. Cummings wants to remodel the house and replace the original garage, but the structure will be located about three feet north of the existing garage and fence. Debbie Walker has protested that the new structures, as described by our client, will be partially built on her property. Cummings has pointed out that the real property line had been located three feet north of the existing garage and fence, but Debbie Walker is attempting to obtain title by claiming adverse possession.

✦EXERCISE 26.F - SUBJECT-VERB AGREEMENT

This exercise should be done after reading Section 26.4.1 in the *Handbook*.

✦Choose the form of the verb that agrees with the subject.

1. All of the justices (was/were) in favor of reviewing the case.

2. There (was/were) no further unexecuted acts to be performed by the landlord.

3. Georgia, as well as nineteen other states, (outlaw/outlaws) all acts of sodomy.

4. Not at issue in this case (is/are) those parts of Section 16-6-2 criminalizing sodomy by force.

5. A majority of the panel (has/have) found that Smith possessed sufficient standing to pursue the action.

6. All of the evidence in this case (is/are) circumstantial.

7. The Respondent, in seeking declaratory and injunctive relief, (claims/claim) that the statute violates his right to privacy under the first, third, fourth, fifth, ninth, and fourteenth amendments to the United States Constitution.

8. Your problem (is/are) seven employees who want a cost of living adjustment added to their retirement benefits.

9. "Known and unknown, foreseen and unforeseen bodily and personal injuries" (was/were) added to the updated version of the medical release form.

10. The appellate court, in exceptional circumstances and as an exception to the rule, (considers/consider) questions not presented to the trial court if they involve a possible denial of due process or if criminal penalties attach.

11. The injuries that Sullivan discovered after she had signed the release (raises/raise) a material issue of fact concerning the validity of the release.

12. Reversing the summary judgment and remanding the case for trial (is/are) the only proper course of action the court can take.

13. The *Finch* case, as well as the *Nellington* case, (is/are) distinguishable from Sullivan's situation.

14. Each nurse and orderly at the station (was/were) in frequent contact with the patients in that wing.

15. Neither the driver nor any of the passengers on the bus (has/have) admitted that the bus veered over the double yellow line.

16. The procedures governing relief from a default judgment (is/are) set forth in CR 60, which allows the court to excuse a party from a judgment for, among other reasons, "mistakes, inadvertence, surprise, excusable neglect or irregularity in obtaining a judgment order." CR 60(b)(1).

17. An affidavit from Grayson's attorney setting forth the procedural history of the case, along with excerpts from depositions of Crowell's supervisors and from Crowell himself, (has/have) been filed in support of the motion.

18. A search of Brown's car turned up a copy of "World Warriors," which (publishes/publish) articles glorifying the violent lives of mercenary soldiers.

19. "Prior unrelated matters" (refer/refers) here to prior convictions.

20. Every door and window to the victim's home (was/were) left unlocked.

✦EXERCISE 26.G PRONOUN AGREEMENT

This exercise should be done after reading Section 26.4.2 in the *Handbook*.

✦Read the following sentences and correct the errors in pronoun agreement. If the sentence has no pronoun agreement errors, mark it "correct."

1. The appellate court upheld the trial court's verdict, stating that they found no manifest abuse of discretion.

2. Under cross-examination, a witness may suddenly realize that their earlier testimony was inaccurate.

3. Someone who makes an obscene telephone call is unlikely to use his real name.

4. Courts interpreting the ECOA's actual damage provision have declared that a successful plaintiff may recover for injury to their credit rating, as well as damages for embarrassment, humiliation, and emotional distress.

5.   When a tax consultant prepares a tax return for a client, they use only what the client gives them.

6.   The police had reason to believe that either Collins or his companions were armed and dangerous based on their alleged involvement in the Bleauville robbery.

7.   The board firmly believed that their main responsibility was to protect Acme Textiles, Inc. from a hostile corporate takeover.

8.   Somebody used their master key to enter the storage room and remove the typewriter.

9.   The parents and their daughter have their hands bound behind their backs.

10. In *Snowadzki*, the IRS successfully argued that they had nothing to do with where or how the records were going to be obtained.

11. In order to assert the sudden emergency doctrine, the party claiming the defense must show that he or she is confronted by a sudden, unexpected peril, through no negligence of their own.

12. Harrison Tractor Company can argue that they were operating in good faith when they signed the agreement.

13. The store detective assumed that either the defendant or her mother must have hidden the bracelet in her purse.

14. When the trial court refused to submit the statutory instruction, it forced the jury to determine their own meaning for the terms "knowingly" and "interest," which may or may not have matched those established by the legislature.

15. The defendant, Jeffrey Lyons, argued that the trial court had no authority to impose a polygraph examination as a condition of his probation because they are unreliable.

16. Everyone living in the apartment complex parks their car in the vacant lot across the street.

17. Neither his team nor his friend is willing to testify about Michael's threats to harm Principal Evans because they believe that those statements were "the drugs, not Michael, talking."

18. Only after the court has concluded that the evidence is relevant can they balance the probative value against the prejudicial effect.

19.   The police report states that the unknown perpetrator of the crime removed a screen and

left his fingerprints on the window.

20.   The Water Rights Registration Act, Wash. Rev. Code §90.14 (1989), required every

person who claimed water rights not evidenced by the 1917 or 1945 water codes to

register their claim with the State before June 30, 1974.

✦EXERCISE 26.H - AMBIGUOUS PRONOUNS

This exercise should be done after reading Section 26.5.1 in the *Handbook.*

✦Revise the following sentences to clarify the ambiguous pronouns.

1.   Howard Davis claims that the apartment manager yelled "Stop!", but he never made an

effort to interfere.

2.   Davidson cooperated in the search by telling the police about the money and plane ticket

under the false bottom of his suitcase. Davidson asserts that it was from a recent

trip to California.

3.   Two brothers, Earl and Mason Hargrove, own two lumber yards, Eastside Building

Supplies and Hargrove Lumber and Hardware. They are both financially stable.

4. O'Brien jammed the coins back behind the car seat and then hid the guns under the spare tire. After a complete search of the vehicle, they were found by Officer Martinez.

5. Juror Marc Stein stated to all other jurors that he had discussed the accident with his brother-in-law, a professional truck driver. He said that the accident could not have occurred as the defendant testified.

6. After giving chase, Officer Conner apprehended Helman, who had a red bandanna scarf wrapped around his hand. It had some glass fragments in it.

7. A claim by Stravinski that he was not present at the scene of the crime is not necessarily antagonistic with a claim by McDonald that he was present but did not commit the crime.

8. After conducting a pat-down search of the defendant, Deputy Peterson found a razor blade wrapped in a tissue under his vehicle.

9. Edna Lino testified that several men, including James Crowell, approached the petitioner after he slapped her. She further testified that he appeared to be afraid that he would beat him up.

10. Clyde Reeves and his son, Daryl, were both injured in two automobile accidents that occurred within two months of each other. The first accident occurred on October 8,

1987, when he was injured in a rear end collision with a vehicle driven by Melvin Maye.
He immediately sought and received medical care for the injuries from Dr. Charles
Santino, his family physician. Later, on November 10, 1987, while still under his care, he
was involved in an accident with a vehicle driven by Carter Szabo. He again sought and
received medical treatment from him.

✦EXERCISE 26.1 - BROAD PRONOUN REFERENCE

This exercise should be done after reading Section 26.5.2 in the *Handbook*.

✦Revise the following sentences to correct the broad pronoun reference.

1. In *Colorado Carpet*, the court held that an oral contract for ordinary carpet was
    unenforceable. The *Colorado Carpet* court reasoned that there was no evidence to
    indicate that the carpet was specially made for the buyer because it could be found in
    other retail outlets. The defendant tried to use this to say that the towels, like the carpet,
    are not special.

2. The defense could bring up evidence of large sales of happy face items during the happy
    face fad several years ago. However, the happy face fad no longer exists, which weakens
    this argument.

3. The defense counsel addressed the subject of silence during direct examination of the defendant, which opened the door for a further development of the subject.

4. The trial court admitted the defendant's prior convictions for theft because they proved only that the defendant acted in conformity with his propensity to commit crimes, which is prohibited by ER 404(b).

5. The destruction of the rosebushes could be classified as permanent, which would make the school district liable for the difference in the value of the Archers' property before and after the damage.

6. The Washington State Constitution expressly forbids the in-court questioning of witnesses about their religious beliefs for the purpose of affecting the weight of their testimony. Wash. Const. art. I, §11. This is repeated and underscored by Washington Rule of Evidence 610.

7. In the instant case, the prosecution asked the prosecuting witness several questions about her religious activities, beliefs, and opinions, bolstering her credibility with the jury at the expense of Mr. Doughtery's due process rights. (RP 151-52). U.S. Const. amend. XIV;

Wash. Const. art. I §22. In allowing this, the trial court committed an error of constitutional magnitude. *See Thomas*, 130 Ariz. at 435, 436 636 P.2d at 1217-18; *Estabrook*, 162 Or. at 101, 91 P.2d at 850.

8. Thus, the prosecution used the witness's religious beliefs, which had nothing to do with the issues before the trial court, to make her testimony seem more credible than Mr. Doughtery's testimony. Such is prohibited under Wash. Const. art I, §11 and ER 610.

9. Under ER 609(a)(2), when a trial court admits prior conviction evidence of a crime that does not contain an element of deceit, fraud, or false swearing, the trial court commits an error of constitutional magnitude. *State v. Harris,* 102 Wash. 2d 148, 685 P.2d 584 (1984). The rationale for this is that while crimes of dishonesty bear directly on a defendant's propensity for truthfulness, other types of crimes do not bear on truthfulness and their admission might serve to prejudice the jury against the defendant.

10. The trial court did not give a cautionary accomplice instruction. This court held that such is required whenever the prosecution relies solely on accomplice testimony.

✦EXERCISE 26.J   PRONOUN ANTECEDENTS

This exercise should be done after reading Section 26.5.3 in the *Handbook*.

◆Revise the following sentences so that all pronouns have noun antecedents.

1.   The Bloomquists' pre-marital agreement states that they consider Mr. Bloomquist's residuals to be community property.

2.   In Freeman's book, *The Grammatical Lawyer*, he discusses numerous rules of usage.

3.   From the board's minutes, we can infer that it knew about the structural weaknesses in the building and decided not to act.

4.   An attorney's notes from a client interview must be protected under the work-product rule; otherwise, the opposition will have access to the strategy he or she plans to use in the case.

5.   According to petitioner's testimony, he did not deliberately shoot anyone.

◆EXERCISE 26.K - PRONOUN REVIEW

This exercise should be done after reading Section 26.5 in the *Handbook.*

◆Correct all the problems with pronouns in the following sentences:

1. In *Finch*, the petitioner's vehicle collided with the respondent's. He submitted a claim for property damage to respondent's insurance carrier, which he agreed to pay.

2. Anita Hempstead is a single mother with an 18-month-old daughter. The lights and noise from the night baseball prevent her from sleeping. This occurs twice a week. Consequently, Ms. Hempstead claims that the loss of sleep interrupts her entire weekly schedule.

3. Upon receipt of Wilson's case, the prosecutor's office treated it in the same fashion as all other referrals. That included processing the police reports, screening them for legal sufficiency, typing and filing an information, and setting an arraignment date with proper notice. Once he realized that it could not be routinely processed in the twelve business days between receipt of the police reports and Wilson's eighteenth birthday, he referred the case to the adult division for filing charges.

4. In May of 1986, the president of Glad Tidings Towel Company (GTT) telephoned the president of Smokey Stover Hotels (SSH) to say that he was now responsible for the order and to inform him that GTT had completed 20,000 of the 50,000 towels ordered. This surprised him because he had never signed a contract ordering the towels, which is company policy.

✦EXERCISE 26.L - MODIFIER PLACEMENT

This exercise should be done after reading Section 26.6.1 in the *Handbook*.

✦Using the single word modifiers in parentheses, move the modifier to several positions in the sentence and explain the resulting change in meaning.

1.   The deputy prosecutor asked that the plaintiff describe his assailant. (JUST)

2.   The defendant claims that the plaintiff was sleeping. (ONLY)

✦EXERCISE 26.M - MODIFIER PLACEMENT

This exercise should be done after reading Section 26.6.1 in the *Handbook*.

✦In the following sentences, decide where the modifiers should be placed.

1.   After Mr. Harper pays alimony and child support, he has enough money to live on.

        (BARELY)

2.   The court stated that the unavoidable accident defense was appropriate when neither party

        was at fault and when the party was surprised by sudden changes in circumstances that

        the party could not reasonably anticipate. (ONLY)

✦Exercise 26.N - Misplaced Modifiers

✦Revise the following sentences to correct the misplaced modifiers.

1. The deputy marshal testified on March 12, 1989, that a copy of the complaint was served on the defendant at his Chicago residence. (Service was on March 12, 1989, not the deputy marshal's statement.)

2. The duty of a plaintiff in a failed vasectomy is only to mitigate damages through a reasonable means; an abortion is not required.

3. The court reasoned that many people would be willing to support the unplanned child given the chance. (Revise so that many people, not the unplanned child, are given the chance.)

4. Acme Clothing Co. discriminated against Mary Smith when it failed to issue her a new credit card for an existing open-ended account under her maiden name. (The account was under her married name; she wants a new credit card under her maiden name.)

5. Custom-made towels ordered by the buyer imprinted with yellow happy faces trimmed in purple satisfy the requirement of specially manufactured goods.

6.   Harrison Lumber Co., the plaintiff in this action, has filed suit against our client, Lloyd Putnam, for breach of contract in federal district court.

7.   Hawaii currently does not restrict foreign investment in privately owned real estate; on the contrary, discrimination is prohibited in real estate transactions based on ancestry.

8.   In *Rovinski v. Rowe*, Robert Rowe brought a personal injury action against Stanley Rovinski for injuries from an automobile accident that he sustained.

9.   Mrs. Davidson's car collided with Mrs. Howe's car in the middle lane, which was traveling at a lawful rate of speed.

10.   Although gruesome, the court held that the photographs must be considered in light of the facts needed to be proved by the prosecution.

✦EXERCISE 26.O - DANGLING MODIFIERS

✦Revise the following sentences to correct for dangling modifiers.

1.   In order to answer this question, the rule that governs service of process must be examined.

2.   Applying the majority rule to our facts, the benefit of the Bells having a healthy child outweighs the burden.

3. To prove discrimination, it must be shown that the only difference between our client and the others granted credit was Ms. Smith's protected classification.

4. In using the balancing test, whether the defendant testified at the prior trial must be considered.

5. Comparing *McDonald* to our case, the facts are conclusive that Komotios's identification in the police car resulted from impermissibly suggestive police actions.

6. To determine whether Acme discriminated against our client, four factors must be examined.

7. In measuring monetary damages to real property, two distinctions are made.

8. In determining what constitutes "appreciable time," a specific or standard amount of time has not been clearly defined by the courts.

9. Equipment designs are presented to the prospective buyer for approval. Once approved, a bid stating the contract price is submitted.

10. In order to collect your pruning fee from Mr. Brown, filing a lien against his orchard may be the best course of action.

✦EXERCISE 26.P -PARALLELISM

This exercise should be done after reading Section 26.7 in the *Handbook*.

✦Revise the following sentences so that the coordinated elements are parallel.

1. The defense counsel elicited that the appellant paid for a listed telephone in his own name, kept some clothes and artifacts there, and the room was ready for him to be occupied.

2. As a result of the collision, Rice suffered a severe concussion, two broken ribs, lost a front tooth, whiplash, and numerous bruises and lacerations.

3. Provisions allowing arbitration are generally upheld because they enhance fair dealing among the parties and for the prevention of litigation.

4. Chavaria's only reasons for breaking into the locked box in the Senator's desk were his suspicion that it contained the Senator's financial records and he expected a probable reward from the Justice Department.

5.   The voluminous record in this case contains both substantial and conflicting evidence regarding the sequence of events, the actions of the parties, and what was the condition of the intersection.

6.   The issues for review are whether the trial court abused its discretion by not placing a value on certain items of personal property and when it ordered John to pay $600 per month in child support for his four children.

7.   One factor governing the award of child support includes the cost of caring for, maintaining, and education of the children.

8.   The two critical factors in the "instrument or agent" analysis of Fourth Amendment search and seizure law are whether the government knew about and acquiesced to the search and the intent of the party performing the search.

9.   Clipse described the assailant as wearing a green denim outfit, glasses, and had short wavy hair.

10.   To ensure that claimants would be aware of the new act, the Legislature directed the Department of Ecology to publish a statutorily prescribed notice by four different means: 1) publication of the notice once a year for five years in major as well as local newspapers; 2) publication of the notice every six months on radio and television stations

broadcasting in every county; 3) posting the notice in a conspicuous location in every county; and 4) including a copy of the notice with notices of taxes due for 1972 mailed by each county treasurer.

◆EXERCISE 26.Q -PARALLELISM

This exercise should be done after reading Section 26.7 in the *Handbook*.

◆Revise the following sentences so that the coordinated elements are parallel.

1.   The trial court concluded that the agreement was not only fair economically but also procedurally fair.

2.   Green fibers that were found to be microscopically indistinguishable from the fibers in Nichol's t-shirt both were found in the car and on the gloves.

3.   Mr. Parker claims that the trial court's actions resulted in a property distribution that was neither fair nor was it equitable.

4.   The plaintiff alleges that the City failed not only to erect proper warning signs but also failed to trim obscuring vegetation at the northeast quadrant of the intersection.

5.   The jury is not to consider this evidence as either proof of negligence or as an admission of negligence on the part of the City.

6. The notation on the agent's copy could mean that either Peters made only a quote to Garfield or actually obtained the excess coverage from Munson Insurance.

7. The State can neither take action that will unnecessarily "chill" the assertion of a constitutional right nor can the State draw adverse inferences from the exercise of a constitutional right.

8. In this case, the prosecutor's comments appear to extend more to the defendant's theory of mistaken identity than his guilt or innocence.

9. The State charged Mookins with one count of assault committed either by the use of a weapon or instrument likely to produce bodily harm or by knowingly inflicting grievous bodily harm upon the victim.

10. Heller did not object to the use of the medical records evidence at either the board hearing or during the trial de novo in superior court.

Chapter 27
Punctuation

The "Quick Overview of the Comma Rules" may be helpful in doing Exercises 27.A - 27.N.

QUICK OVERVIEW OF THE COMMA RULES

♦ *CRITICAL COMMAS: those that affect meaning and clarity*

Rule 1:

Use a comma before a coordinating conjunction joining two main clauses.

Example: The prosecutor spoke about the defendant's motive, and the jury listened carefully.

Rule 2:

Use a comma to set off long introductory phrases or clauses from the main clause.

Example: Using their overhead lights and sirens, the police followed the defendant out of the area.

Rule 3:

Use a comma to prevent a possible misreading.

Example: At the time, the prosecution informed Jones that it would recommend a sentence of 18 months.

Rule 4:

Use a comma to set off nonrestrictive phrases or clauses.

    Example: Officer Bates, acting as a decoy, remained outside on the sidewalk.

✦*BASIC COMMAS: those that educated readers expect·*

Rule 5:

Set off nonrestrictive appositives with commas.

    Example: A corrections officer called Diane Cummins, the defendant's girlfriend.

Rule 6:

Set off nonrestrictive participial phrases with a comma or commas.

    Example: The trial court denied the motion, finding that the seizure fell under the plain view doctrine.

Rule 7:

Use a comma or commas to set off transitional or interrupting words and phrases.

    Example: The trial court, however, imposed an exceptional sentence of 30 months.

Rule 8:

Use commas according to convention with quotation marks.

    Example: Corbin said, "I never saw the other car."

Rule 9:

Use a comma or commas to set off phrases of contrast.

>   *Example*:   Adams initially indicated that he, not Wilson, was involved in the robbery.

Rule 10:

Use commas between items in a series.

>   *Example*:   Wong had no money, identification, or jewelry.

Rule 11:

Use a comma between coordinate adjectives not joined by a conjunction.

>   *Example*:   The contract was written in concise, precise language.

Rule 12:

Use commas according to convention with dates, addresses, and names of geographical locations.

>   *Example*:   The land in Roswell, New Mexico, was surveyed on October 4, 1986, and purchased less than a month later.

◆*ESOTERIC COMMAS: those that are required in sophisticated sentence structures*

Rule 13:

Use commas to set off absolutes.

>   *Example*:   His career destroyed, Williams lapsed into a state of depression.

Rule 14:

Use a comma to indicate an omission of a word or words that can be understood from the context.

Example: The first witness said the attacker was "hairy"; the second, bald.

Rule 15:

Use commas to set off expressions that introduce examples or explanations.

Example: Collins testified that Adams had participated in the robbery and had fenced some of the items, namely, a camera, stereo, and silver.

✦*UNNECESSARY COMMAS: those that should be omitted*

Rule 16:

Do not use a comma to set off restrictive adverbial clauses that follow the main clause.

Example: Complicity may be found if a defendant participates in the early stages of an activity that results in the attack on the victim.

Rule 17:

Do not use a comma to separate a subject from its verb or a verb from its object.

Example: The idea that an individual can obtain another person's property through adverse possession is difficult for many people to accept.

Rule 18:

Do not use a comma to separate correlative pairs unless the correlatives introduce main clauses.

> *Example*:   Neither the United States Supreme Court nor this court has ever ruled that a defendant has a due process right to an instruction on lesser included offenses.

*Rule 19:

Do not use a comma between a conjunction and introductory modifiers or clauses.

> *Example*:   The fire had completely destroyed the trailer, and according to the fire chief, there was some concern that the overhead structure of the barn would collapse.

*Rule 20:

Do not use a comma between *that* and introductory modifiers or clauses.

> *Example*:   He testified that when they returned to his hotel room, Wells demanded a $150 fee.

* Some authorities disagree on these comma rules.

◆EXERCISE 27.A -COMMAS

This exercise should be done after reading Section 27.1.1 (Rule 1) in the *Handbook*.

✦Add commas as needed in the following sentences.

1. McNeill was initially represented by counsel but he moved for a court-appointed attorney shortly before trial.

2. The trial court did not abuse its discretion in allowing a uniformed deputy to be present in the courtroom and the petitioner has not shown any prejudice stemming from the exercise of this discretion.

3. McNair admitted at the sentencing hearing that the victim was four years old and that he was 21 but he disputed the court's other reasons for the exceptional sentence.

4. The record of the 1986 guilty plea hearing reflects that Wadsworth was incarcerated at the time of his attempted escape and that he understood the elements of the escape charge and its possible punishment.

5. Numerous people complained to Dr. Pao about the billing practices yet he expressed his approval and encouraged continuation of the practices.

6.   The defendant's associates are known to have Mafia connections and one has a reputation

for deadly violence.

7.   Olmsted was aware of the charges against him and the record reflects that he knowingly

waived his constitutional rights before entering a guilty plea.

8.   The cocaine's wholesale value was $17,000 and its street value was $80,000.

9.   The invasion of Jones's rights appears to be minimal for it was Jones herself who directed

the officer to retrieve the identification from her purse.

10.   The president of Clearwater Mutual Savings Association demanded that the *Times* print a

retraction of the false story but the *Times* refused to do so.

✦EXERCISE 27.B - COMMAS

This exercise should be done after reading Section 27.1.1 (Rule 2) in the *Handbook.*

> **Rule 2:**
>
> **Use a comma to set off long introductory phrases or clauses from the main clause**.

✦Add commas as needed in the following sentences.

1.   To convict the defendant of the crime charged the court must find that he had actual

      knowledge that he was possessing stolen property.

2.   In response to DuPont's request Hommel agreed to accompany DuPont to the rear of the

      store.

3.   Viewing the evidence in a light most favorable to the prosecution the trial court found the

      essential elements of the crime.

4.   In the early morning hours of December 3, 1983 officers from the Houston Police

      Department were dispatched to an abandoned railroad depot.

5.   Furthermore the trial court cautioned the jury to scrutinize separately each defendant's

      case.

6.   Moreover to ensure that claimants would be aware of the new act the legislature directed

      the Department of Ecology to publish a statutorily prescribed notice.

7.   When the police conduct a search without a warrant the state must prove that the

      particular search or seizure falls with one of the "jealously and carefully guarded"

      exceptions to the warrant requirement. *Arkansas v. Sanders*, 442 U.S. 753 (1979).

8.   In *Beck* the United States Supreme Court held that the death sentence may not

constitutionally be imposed for a capital offense when the jury was not permitted to

consider any lesser included offenses.

9.   After waiving his right to a speedy trial six times Martin pleaded guilty to the crime of

indecent liberties.

10.   However if the evidence is admissible for one of these purposes the trial court must

determine whether the danger of undue prejudice from its admission outweighs the

probative value of the evidence.

✦EXERCISE 27.C   COMMAS

This exercise should be done after reading Section 27.1.1 (Rule 3) in the *Handbook.*

Rule 3:
Use a comma to prevent a possible misreading.

✦Using rule 3, add commas as needed.

1.   Of the twenty two witnesses are willing to testify.

2.   During a surveillance on three successive evenings police officers observed people

exchanging cash for packaged articles.

3. Two years before the car's brakes failed on a steep mountain road.

4. Once he had the idea that all women were laughing at him behind his back.

5. Without a doubt about half the witnesses to the accident will be unwilling to get involved.

◆EXERCISE 27.D - COMMAS

This exercise should be done after reading Section 27.1.1. (Rule 4) in the *Handbook*.

Rule 4:			
Use a comma to set off nonrestrictive phrases or clauses.			
Restrictive	restricts word it modifies	no commas	who/whom that
Nonrestrictive	does not restrict word it modifies	commas	who/whom which

◆Add commas as needed in the following sentences.

1. Trooper Yessler who investigated the accident testified that the "primary causal factor" of the accident was Neimeyer's intoxicated state.

2. The state trooper who investigated the accident testified that the "primary causal factor" of the accident had been Neimeyer's intoxicated state.

3. The legislature enacted the Water Rights Registration Act which required every person who claimed water rights not evidenced by the 1917 or 1945 water codes to register a claim with the State before June 30, 1974.

4. The police talked with a neighbor who had seen a man matching Daniels's description within a block of the Wyatt home on the day of the burglary.

5. At about 10:30 p.m., Officer Underwood encountered Norman Rhemn whom she had observed driving by several times during the evening.

6. Did the trial court err in giving instruction 9 which sets forth the circumstances permitting the jury to find whether the petitioner had "actual knowledge" that he possessed stolen property?

7. Those who fail to file waive their water rights.

8. The defendant's conviction was reversed on the ground that the informant was a material witness who could not be subpoenaed by the defense. *Id.* at 1146.

9. The State appealed to Division Two of the Court of Appeals which reversed and remanded in a published opinion filed August 5, 1986.

10. A polygraph examination is a reasonable extension of those statutory conditions that require a probationer to follow the instructions of his or her probation officer. See, for example, Wash. Rev. Code 9.95.210.

✦EXERCISE 27.E - COMMAS

This exercise should be done after reading Section 27.1.1 (Rule 4) in the *Handbook*.

Rule 4:

Use a comma to set off nonrestrictive phrases or clauses.

Restrictive	restricts word it modifies	no commas	who/whom that
Nonrestrictive	does not restrict word it modifies	commas	who/whom which

◆Explain the difference in meaning in the following pairs of sentences.

1a.   Barley & Barnes argued that independent contractors who performed the actual dredging were responsible for any negligence.

b.   Barley & Barnes argued that independent contractors, who performed the actual dredging, were responsible for any negligence.

2a.   Defense counsel will discuss all of the factors that favor exclusion of prior conviction evidence.

b.   Defense counsel will discuss all of the factors, which favor exclusion of prior conviction evidence.

3a.   Based on that information, the detectives checked for the serial number, which was

missing.

b.   Based on that information, the detectives checked for the serial number that was missing.

✦EXERCISE 27.F - COMMAS

This exercise should be done after reading Section 27.1.2 (Rules 5 and 6) in the *Handbook*.

Rule 5:

Set off nonrestrictive appositives with commas.

Rule 6:

Set off nonrestrictive participial phrases with a comma or commas.

✦Using rules 5 and 6, add commas as needed.

1.   The State has charged the defendant with dealing in a controlled substance a Class B

felony.

2.   The State opposed the motion arguing that the defendant should have filed a personal

restraint petition.

3.   The only witness Ann Peters had discussed her potential criminal liability with the

prosecutor.

4.   Contending that his prior guilty pleas were constitutionally invalid Lemons moved to vacate the remaining habitual criminal order.

5.   Petitioner Christopher Landa seeks review of a Court of Appeals decision affirming his conviction for second degree burglary.

6.   Olson claims that a new trial should have been granted because Nyles the victim was available to testify.

7.   Supreme Court Justices Brennan and Scalia voted against granting certiorari.

8.   Campbell's most recent conviction was for second-degree assault the same crime he is currently charged with committing.

9.   Holding that the facts were sufficient to require the submission of the defense of duress to the jury the Court of Appeals reversed stating that "[t]he time has come when we can no longer close our eyes to the growing problem of institutional gang rapes in our prison system."

10. Olsen appealed to the Court of Appeals assigning error to the fact that the trial court permitted "the presence of uniformed deputies in the courtroom." See App. brief, at 6.

✦EXERCISE 27.G - COMMAS

This exercise should be done after reading Section 27.1.2 (Rules 7 and 8) in the *Handbook.*

Rule 7:

Use a comma or commas to set off transitional or interrupting words and phrases.

Rule 8:

Use commas according to convention with quotation marks.

✦Using rules 7 and 8, add commas as needed.

1. When asked whether he and O'Malley were aware that Tanner had a gun, Swanson replied "Sure."

2. One could infer therefore that the billing procedures were there for her to see.

3. If your answers to both of these questions is "yes" then the defendant was negligent.

4. The evidence is admissible under ER 402, which states that "[a]ll relevant evidence is admissible . . . ."

5. Roberts however asserts that she was amenable to process at all times.

6. Other cases on the other hand suggest that the evidence necessary to satisfy the second prong of the *Workman* test may come from any source.

7. The trial court concluded that "Zeblowski was not so intoxicated that he did not comprehend or intend his acts."

8. The trial court concluded "Zeblowski was not so intoxicated that he did not comprehend or intend his acts."

9. An appellate court may on its own initiative or by motion of a party request additional evidence before rendering a decision on a case.

10. In *Alford*, the United States Supreme Court held that a plea of guilty is constitutionally valid in spite of a defendant's claim of innocence when there was strong evidence of guilt before the trial court and when the plea was a voluntary and an intelligent choice among the alternative courses of action open to a defendant. *North Carolina v. Alford, supra*, at 37-38.

✦Exercise 27.H Commas

This exercise should be done after reading Section 27.1.2 (Rules 9 and 10) in the *Handbook*.

Rule 9:
Use a comma or commas to set off phrases of contrast.

Rule 10:
Use commas between items in a series.

✦Using rules 9 and 10, add commas as needed.

1. Yesler later identified James in a photo montage in a lineup and at trial.

2. The evidence shows that the defendant was only present at the crime scene not "ready to assist."

3. The prosecutor's comment of disbelief was directed at the defense theory of mistaken identity not at the credibility of a witness.

4. Thompson pulled his gun held it straight up in the air and told Lew not to bring anyone back.

5. Thus, the 90-day "time for trial" rule under CrR 3.3(c)(1) began to run when Lewis was arraigned not when the State filed the information.

6.   The sanity commission concluded that Thomas was incapable of perceiving the nature of his conduct at the time of the offense was unable to distinguish right from wrong but was competent to stand trial.

7.   The court must follow United States Supreme Court decisions not a decision by the New Mexico Court of Appeals when determining whether a defendant is a public or private figure.

8.   The *Harris* court held that such an instruction is required whenever the prosecution relies solely on accomplice testimony but that failure to give the instruction is not reversible error when there is sufficient corroborating testimony.

9.   Chavez saw a man on the ground but was unable to identify him because of the darkness.

10.   Jeffreys was arrested for armed robbery yet was also charged later with second degree burglary.

✦EXERCISE 27.I - COMMAS

This exercise should be done after reading Section 27.1.2 (Rule 11 and 12) in the *Handbook*.

Rule 11:

Use a comma between coordinate adjectives not joined by a conjunction.

Rule 12:

Use commas according to convention with dates, addresses, and names of geographical locations.

◆Using rules 11 and 12, add commas as needed. Revise sentences if necessary.

1.   She was taken into custody on May 11 1987 and arraigned on May 12 1987.

2.   The documents in question mysteriously disappeared from the Dallas office on December 2 1987 only to reappear in the Clovis New Mexico office on December 9.

3.   Bennett purchased twelve acres of remote undeveloped land in central Florida in 1977.

4.   Secret unexpressed intentions are irrelevant.

5.   Each applicant was required to enclose a self-addressed stamped envelope with the application form.

6.   Johnston moved to Las Vegas Nevada in February 1986 to attend school.

7.   The publisher mailed the contract on 1 March 1989 to the author at her Cincinnati Ohio address.

8.	"Substantial evidence" exists if it is "sufficient to persuade a fair-minded rational person of the truth of the declared premise." See *Holland v. Boeing Co.*, 90 Wash. 2d 384, 390-91, 583 P.2d 621, 624 (1978).

9.	Peterson filed his motion to vacate on October 26 1983 more than two years after the trial court entered the judgment of acquittal.

10.	People who received one of these letters were told to "mail $5.00 to the last name and address on the list," which was Amy Andersen 1813 South Washington Lawrence Kansas 66044, or they would suffer "bad luck and other misfortune."

✦EXERCISE 27.J - COMMAS

This exercise should be done after reading Section 27.1.3 (Rules 13, 14, and 15) in the *Handbook*.

Rule 13:

Use commas to set off absolutes.

Rule 14:

Use a comma to indicate an omission of a word or words that can be understood from the context.

Rule 15:

Use commas to set off expressions that introduce examples or explanations.

◆Using rules 13, 14, and 15, add commas as needed.

1.   The white envelope contained 100 hits of acid; the blue another 100 hits.

2.   A jury entered two habitual criminal findings each based on the same prior convictions.

3.   The prosecutor has two choices in cases such as Jerome's namely proceed under Wash. Rev. Code 9.94A.125 and 9.94A.310 by charging possession of a firearm and, upon a finding to that effect, increase the presumptive range by 12 months or not charge possession of a firearm and seek an exceptional sentence under Wash. Rev. Code 9.94A.390(4)(d).

4.   The adverse claimant must assert possession in a "hostile" manner; that is he or she must assert the claim against all others, including the owner of record.

5.   A person who dies intestate--that is without a valid will--leaves his or her family a legacy of woe.

6.   Melvin Andersen is listed as the president of the corporation; Philip Andersen the vice-president of operations; Teresa Andersen the vice-president of internal affairs, and Mary Andersen the treasurer.

7.   Her only source of income cut off Irene Culver had no choice but to return to the street.

8.   McGurk's will did not specify heirs for numerous valuable possessions *e.g.* a three-carat

       diamond, 1500 shares of IBM, a 110 foot yacht, and a Rolls Royce.

9.   Her surgery having been labeled "successful" Glenda Jefferson checked out of the

       hospital and returned home.

10.   The person made four identical calls the first less than two hours after the incident.

✦EXERCISE 27.K - UNNECESSARY COMMAS

This exercise should be done after reading Section 27.1.4 (Rule 16) in the *Handbook*.

Rule 16:

Do not use a comma to set off restrictive adverbial clauses that follow the main clause.

✦Using Rule 16, omit unnecessary commas in the following sentences. If a comma is needed, add it.

1.   A statute of frauds defense can be raised, if the employment contract is determined to

       have a definite term and if the contract cannot be performed within a year.

2.   Plaintiff's motion for summary judgment should be denied, when a genuine issue of

       material fact exists.

3. The court will hold that the contract is void because the parole evidence will satisfy the statute of frauds requirement.

4. The light fixture shattered and fell, as Pearson entered the room.

5. An employer can be liable in tort for wrongful discharge if the employee's discharge contravenes a clear mandate of public policy." *Id.*

6. There is circumstantial evidence to support the fact that Dr. Deaver encouraged fraudulent billing practices although there is no direct evidence connecting him to those practices.

7. Ramparts, Inc. will immediately release the documents requested, unless the court enjoins such an action.

8. A defendant does not act improperly when the defendant has a financial interest in the business of the person induced.

9. The plaintiff is unlikely to succeed in her defamation claim, because the defendant's statement was true and because the statement does not have defamatory meaning.

10. In both *LeFever* and *Dowling*, this court held that the retrial of a defendant is barred when a trial court dismisses a case for insufficient evidence even though that ruling may be erroneous.

✦EXERCISE 27.L UNNECESSARY COMMAS

This exercise should be done after reading Section 27.1.4 (Rules 17-20) in the *Handbook*.

Rule 17:

Do not use a comma to separate a subject from its verb or a verb from its object.

Rule 18:

Do not use a comma to separate correlative pairs unless the correlatives introduce main clauses.

---

*Rule 19:

Do not use a comma between a conjunction and introductory modifiers or clauses.

---

*Rule 20:

Do not use a comma between *that* and introductory modifiers or clauses.

✦Using Rules 17, 18, 19, and 20, delete unnecessary commas in the following sentences. If necessary, revise a sentence.

1. The police put a "trap" on the phone, so, when the man called the next day, the police were able to trace the call.

2. The Hoffelmeirs will probably receive not only the replacement value of the cat, but also compensation for their mental anguish.

3. Defendants may argue that, precisely because the plaintiff operates its business in the small community of Lincoln, it holds a position of special prominence in that community sufficient to make it an all purpose public figure.

4. The intensity of the fire, the danger of injury from the propane tanks, and the condition and construction of the barn, mean that the fire could reasonably be classified as "manifestly dangerous."

5. The *Barr* decision is entitled to much weight in Washington both because it was decided by the full bench of the Washington Supreme Court, and because there was no dissenting opinion.

6. Either she stole the car from the parking lot, or she mistook it for a friend's car.

7. Wells's claim that he was denied his right to cross-examine the representatives of the third-party payors who testified about the payment restrictions, could be valid if he was prevented from negating any inference that he knew the billings were fraudulent.

8.   The court held that, when there is a period of delay between filing the information and the arraignment, the time for trial set forth in CrR 3.3(c)(1) begins to run the date the information is filed.

9.   The court ruled that, although the form was incorrect, the substantive information supplied by the claimant met the legislative intent by "providing adequate records for administration of the state's waters and notifying the State that the water was being put to beneficial use." *Id.* at 704.

10.   Neither did the trial court abuse its discretion, nor did it err in admitting photographs of the defendant with dental retractors in his mouth.

✦EXERCISE 27.M - COMMA REVIEW

This exercise should be done after reading Section 27.1 in the *Handbook.*

✦Using all the comma rules, add or delete commas in the following sentences.

1.   The Supreme Court held that summary judgment was proper, because the State's actions in failing to perform the eye examination, and noting an appropriate restriction were totally unrelated to the accident.

2.   At the disposition hearing, the State presented a document describing Nowell's prior criminal history which consisted of twelve burglary convictions and two minor offenses subject to diversion.

3.   After checking into the Ramada Inn on Highway 12, Gates called Dates Unlimited, an escort service, and arranged for Teresa Mitton to meet him at his hotel room.

4.   Both contentions will fail, if this accident resulted without any warning of Ms. O'Toole's impending blackout.

5.   For example, if Acme conditioned employment on Mr. McIntyre participating in an illegal scheme to fix prices, plaintiff may ultimately succeed in a wrongful discharge claim. *See, e.g., Lanery v. Atlantic Richfield Co.*, 164 Cal. Rptr. 839, 610 P.2d 1330.

6.   Even though the evidence does not demonstrate that Marvin and Leroy verbalized any plan to carry out the assault they both appear to have been active participants in the crime.

7.   The first instance of alleged prosecutorial misconduct occurred during closing argument, when the prosecutor made several statements concerning Toole's failure to call Doris Simms as an alibi witness.

175

8. Owens asserts that the manufacture of a controlled substance may be accomplished only by extraction or chemical synthesis not by cultivation.

9. On the evening of February 28 1977 Atlanta Police Officer, Louise Simpson, was working undercover on prostitution detail.

10. A waiver to the right to a jury trial must be voluntary, knowing and intelligent.

11. Kevin Morton rode as the "spotter", the person designated to alert the boat driver when the skier falls.

12. Defense counsel chose to present only one alibi witness, Bertha Owens, who stated that she was in Des Moines, Iowa at the time of the robbery.

13. Marie Tao, the defendant's girlfriend, was contacted by an officer who asked if the defendant was there but she denied knowing anything about his location.

14. Mason maintains that, like the convictions in *Mace*, one of his convictions was reversed on appeal, and that the habitual criminal finding must likewise be vacated.

15. The Barkers argue that, even if the statutory notice is constitutionally adequate they substantially complied with the requirements of the Water Rights Registration Act.

16. Sanchez argues in his petition for review both that the State did not have probable cause to arrest him for armed robbery without a warrant and that it could not later charge him with second degree burglary.

17. When Officer Smith asked who had been driving the cars Pinette approached him and said "I'm the driver of the Volvo."

18. This court has warned prosecutors that it will not tolerate the admission of repetitious inflammatory photographs.

19. The Washington State Supreme Court has held that, when a case has been appealed and a judgment issued by the appellate court the trial court may not interfere "by any proceeding in the cause which is not directed by the appellate order." *State v. Graeber,* 49 Wash. 2d 874, 875, 307 P.2d 563, 563 (1957).

20. The appellant placed her daughter in a private out-of district school in Denver Colorado without first notifying the school district.

✦EXERCISE 27.N COMMA REVIEW

This exercise should be done after reading Section 27.1 in the *Handbook.*

✦Using all the comma rules in this section, add the necessary commas to the following paragraphs.

1.   To determine whether the comments of a prosecutor denied petitioner a fair trial a

court must first determine if the comments are improper. If they are improper a court

must then consider if there was a "substantial likelihood" that the comments affected the

jury. *State v. Reed*, 102 Wash. 2d 140, 684 P.2d 699 (1984). The "substantial likelihood"

inquiry is premised upon the notion that although a defendant has a constitutional right to

a trial by an impartial jury he or she is not guaranteed an error-free trial. *Id.* at 145; *State

v. Davenport*, 100 Wash. 2d 757, 762, 675 P.2d 1213, 1216 (1984).

2.   In 1979 the legislature opened a four-month window during which any claimant

who missed the prior deadline could register a claim. The Barkers however failed to take

advantage of this window. In 1980 when the Department of Ecology adjudicated the

water rights in the Mohawk Creek Basin the referee concluded that the Barkers had lost

their water rights. The Barkers objected to the referee's decision but to no avail so they

then appealed to Division Three of the Court of Appeals. The Department of Ecology

responded by filing a motion on the merits which the Commissioner granted in a ruling

dated July 18 1985. A motion to modify the Commissioner's ruling was denied on

September 15 1985.

3.   Several days later two detectives assigned to the case drove to a woodcutting site

near Vancouver Washington to contact Hugh Sanders the man in question. They found

Sanders identified themselves and explained their business. RP. 22-23. As they were

speaking to Sanders the detectives noticed a chainsaw on the ground in front of him.
Detective Riley who owned a Husqvarna chainsaw and was generally familiar with that
brand noticed that the saw had the Husqvarna logo on it that it appeared to have been
painted red and that its true orange color was showing through in several places. RP. 25.
When questioned Sanders told the detectives that the chainsaw was a Homelite not a
Husqvarna. He added that "they had no right to touch a man's property." Nevertheless
Detective Riley picked up the chainsaw examined it and noticed that the serial number
plate had been removed. RP. 25-26. The detectives seized the chainsaw and arrested
Sanders who was subsequently charged with possession of stolen property.

4. As the Court of Appeals observed the trial transcript contains only a brief
dialogue concerning Bell's representation by counsel and the pretrial hearings which most
likely would have addressed Bell's request for appointed counsel have not been
transcribed. Thus the record is silent on why an attorney was appointed to represent Bell
and whether Bell validly waived his right to counsel. Without these portions of the
record the Court of Appeals could not have fully considered Bell's claim of self-
representation.

✦EXERCISE 27.O SEMICOLONS

This exercise should be done after reading Section 27.2 (Rule 1) in the *Handbook*.

✦Substitute semicolons for commas or periods separating main clauses when it would be correct
and effective to do so.

1. Thorndike's permission to use his land was an oral license, therefore, he has the right to revoke the license to use his property.

2. Permission is a revokable act, it does not ripen into a prescriptive right unless the user's acts evidence a positive assertion of a right to use. ·

3. Duckworth neither asked for nor received permission. Therefore, his use was adverse to the true owners of the property.

4. Texas law would probably affirm Thorndike's oral license, however, there are incidents in which oral licenses have become prescriptive easements.

5. Duckworth will contend that he offered Thorndike the cord of firewood as consideration in return for the right to use the road. Thorndike will contend that his acceptance of the firewood was not intended as acceptance of consideration.

6. Neither court held for the defendant, neither court was reversed.

7. The police found a tire bar and a paper bag hidden under the house. Both had traces of blood and human hair.

8. The plaintiff's behavior was observable, he was seen actively using the boat.

180

9.   Loren and Joseph assert that the jury linked their actions together because they are

       cousins, therefore, their mutually antagonistic defenses made severance appropriate.

10.   In *Ruona*, the defendant's car was partially in a traffic lane. In *Taylor*, the defendant's car

       was in a borrow pit, which is a trench alongside the road.

✦EXERCISE 27.P SEMICOLONS

This exercise should be done after reading Section 27.2 (Rule 2) in the *Handbook*.

✦Decide which of the following sentences are punctuated correctly and which need a semicolon
rather than a comma between the main clauses.

1.   The first two elements are satisfied, the third element, hostility, is not satisfied.

2.   The first two elements are satisfied, but the third element, hostility, is not satisfied.

3.   The first two elements are satisfied, however, the third element, hostility, is not satisfied.

4.   Although the first two elements are satisfied, the third element, hostility, is not satisfied.

5.   The first two elements are satisfied; the third element, however, is not satisfied.

6.	Thus, if Jones was acting as a private individual, the evidence he obtained will be admitted; if, however, the court finds requisite government involvement in the search, the evidence may be suppressed.

7.	The Justice Department will argue that Jones was acting as a private individual; therefore, the evidence he obtained should be admitted. If the court finds requisite government involvement in the search; however, the evidence will be suppressed.

8.	If Jones was acting as a private individual, then the evidence he obtained will be admitted, however, if the court finds requisite involvement in the search, then the evidence may be suppressed.

9.	Although the evidence Jones obtained may be admitted if he was acting as a private individual, the court will probably find that he acted as a government agent and that there was requisite government involvement in the search; therefore, the evidence probably will be suppressed.

10.	The evidence Jones obtained will be admitted only if he was acting as a private individual; the evidence will be suppressed only if the court finds requisite involvement in the search.

◆EXERCISE 27.Q - SEMICOLONS

This exercise should be done after reading Section 27.2 in the *Handbook*.

◆Replace commas with semicolons in the following sentences if the items in the series are long or if one or more of the items has internal commas.

1. The reasonableness test includes several factors: the location of the business, the degree of interference with another business, and the test of sensibilities, that is, whether a person of ordinary sensibilities would be offended.

2. Remedies for private nuisance include abatement by warrant, injunctions, damages, which are measured by the loss suffered by the plaintiff, or declaratory judgment.

3. The court used several factors in its balancing test: the character of the neighborhood, the ratio of complaining to noncomplaining tenants, and the possible interference with the tenants' comfortable enjoyment of life, with their right to privacy, and with their use of the property as an apartment.

4. Unreasonable use includes uses not authorized by statute, uses not consistent with the character of the neighborhood, and uses not in the public interest.

5. The defendant will point to the following facts to prove he is operating his business lawfully: 1) he has satisfied all necessary zoning and licensing requirements, including the special requirements imposed by the waterfront commission, 2) the fitness club's

activities do not physically invade Harborview restaurant, and 3) the activities do not harm anybody.

6. The fitness club has several options: offer aerobics only in the winter, offer aerobics only in the morning, modify the interior of the club to accommodate aerobics inside, or risk a lawsuit from neighboring businesses.

7. The driver was forced to take one of these actions: 1) slam on the brakes in hopes of stopping before she hit the moving car, 2) swerve her vehicle to the left onto the median, or 3) swerve her vehicle to the right into a parallel lane of traffic.

8. Hopwood will try to establish that Linwood is in the best position to help resolve the situation, that Linwood has refused to help, despite Hopwood's repeated requests for help, and that Linwood's refusal amounts to omission of duty.

9. Three elements of the statute must be examined:

    1) the driver must be intoxicated;

    2) the driver must be in actual physical control of a motor vehicle, and

    3) the motor vehicle must be on a public highway.

10. Under Okla. Stat. Ann. Tit. 47 §11-902 (West Supp. 1984-1985), was defendant in actual

physical control of a motor vehicle while intoxicated under the following circumstances:

1)   defendant was legally intoxicated,

2)   defendant was asleep outside the car,

3)   the vehicle was stalled in the lefthand lane on.a four lane highway, and

4)   the keys were in the ignition, but the engine was off?

✦EXERCISE 27.R - SEMICOLON REVIEW

This exercise should be done after reading Section 27.2 in the *Handbook*.

✦Read the following sentences and decide whether the underlined punctuation is correct as is or whether it should be changed. If correct, simply mark the sentence "correct." If changes in punctuation are required, indicate what punctuation marks should be used.

1.   A true emergency did exist, consequently, there was no time for deliberation.

2.   The viability of a fetus is based on several factors: the health of the mother and child, the

weight and race of the fetus, available life-sustaining techniques, and the length of the

pregnancy, when the length can be determined.

3.   In *Green*, the court refused to rule as a matter of law that a fourteen-week-old fetus was

non-viable; because the court held that viability was a factual issue that must be decided

by a jury.

4. In a similar case, a defendant's failure to signal his intention to make a left hand turn violated the turn signal statute; but the defendant was not liable for the accident because the speed of the other car, not the defendant's failure to signal, was found to be the proximate cause of the accident.

5. Whether to award damages is entirely up to the court's discretion, the court has the option of awarding attorneys' fees to the party who wins the case, but it is not obligated to do so.

6. The jury will find that Mr. Cutter's assessment of the situation was reasonable, therefore, he was not negligent.

7. If these elements are not met, the plaintiff could not maintain an action under public nuisance, but he could still consider a cause of action under private nuisance, which is broadly defined as "every nuisance not included in the definition" of public nuisance.

8. Private nuisance affects the rights of a limited community. Public nuisance affects the rights of the entire community.

9. The Washington Supreme Court has addressed the issue of injury and wrongful death of a fetus and allowed recovery for both; recovery, however, has always been for a "viable fetus."

10. To seize evidence under the plain view doctrine, police officers must satisfy the following requirements:

   1) they must have "prior justification for intrusion";

   2) they must come across the evidence "inadvertently";

   3) they must immediately recognize "that they have evidence before them."

◆EXERCISE 27.S   SEMICOLON REVIEW

This exercise should be done after reading Section 27.2 in the *Handbook*.

◆Read the following section from a legal memorandum. Decide which of the underlined punctuation marks are correct and which should be changed to semicolons.

Under the family car or purpose doctrine, the plaintiffs are entitled to recover damages
                                        1
for the wrongful death of their fetus from the car owner. This doctrine holds the car owner liable

for any damages that result from the use of his automobile by a member of his household. The
                                                                                    2
family car or purpose doctrine is not derived from statute, nevertheless, it is well supported by
                                                                3
Washington case law. *McGinn v. Kimmel*, 36 Wash. 2d 786, 221 P.2d 467 (1950); *Hanford v*
                                                                                    4
Goehry, 24 Wash. 2d 859, 167 P.2d 678 (1946); *Dillon v. Burnett*, 197 Wash. 371, 85 P.2d
                                                5
656 (1938); *Hart v. Hogan*, 173 Wash. 598, 24 P.2d 99 (1933); *Birch v. Abercrombie*, 74
    6   7
Wash. 486, 133 P. 1020 (1913); *Cameron v. Downs*, 32 Wash. App. 875, 650 P.2d 260 (1982).
              8
The family car or purpose doctrine is based on an agency relationship between the owner

of a car and the members of his household. Typically, the car owner buys the car for the
                                                    9
use of all family members, so household members are considered agents when they drive his

187

10

car. To recover damages under the family car or purpose doctrine, one must prove the

11

following four elements:

> 1)   the parent owns, provides or maintains the car,
>
> **12**
>
> 2)   the car is for the customary conveyance of family members and for other family business;
>
> **13**
>
> 3)   at the time of the accident, the car was being driven by a member of the
>
> **14**
>
>   family for whom the car is maintained, and
>
> **15**
>
> 4)   the parent has given either express or implied consent that the family member may drive the car.

Cameron v. Downs, 32 Wash. App. 875, 879-80, 650 P.2d 260, 262-63 (1982).

✦EXERCISE 27.T - COLONS

This exercise should be done after reading Section 27.3 in the *Handbook.*

✦In the following sentences, add or delete colons as needed. If the sentence is correct, simply mark it as correct.

1.   A two-part inquiry is used to determine reliability 1) was the confrontation procedure suggestive, and 2) under the totality of circumstances, was the identification reliable even if the confrontation procedure was suggestive?

2.   Officials who are accorded absolute immunity seem to share one common characteristic they make discretionary decisions in an adversarial proceeding under time and information constraints.

3. In California, the service-oriented businesspersons subject to the bulk sales law are the baker, the cafe or restaurant owner, the garage owner, and the cleaner and dyer.

4. By requiring independent corroborating evidence only in Miranda situations, the court has adopted what seems to be a radical approach admissions made in a pre-Miranda setting, at least in DWI cases, do not need corroborating evidence.

5. The defendant is accused of assaulting Agnes Miller, Denise Donovan, Ellie Emory, and Christine Fremont.

6. The court found that the prosecutor's comments during closing argument were not improper because (1) the witness was "peculiarly available" to the defendant and would have been able to elucidate the events of the crime; (2) the witness has pleaded guilty to a prior crime on the condition that he would not be prosecuted for the crimes charged; and (3) the defendant repeatedly attempted to place responsibility for the charged incident on the witness. *Id.* at 628.

7. An investigation revealed that five individuals were at the railroad depot on the night Jones was assaulted; Francis O'Connor, Noel O'Connor, Phillip Whalen, Paul Mendoza, and Tony Rialto.

8. The trial court gave the following reasons justifying the exceptional sentence:

(1)   The defendant has been in and out of the criminal justice system since the mid 1960s.

(2)   Even while under probation, the defendant has committed crime after crime, which is an affront to the court's purpose of protecting the public and ensuring the protection of law.

(3)   The defendant is a danger to society through his theft and burglary of the property of others and possession of firearms while under felony convictions.

(4)   Probation is not a viable alternative; while under probation, the defendant has continued to commit felonies. CP. 14.

9.   In *Petersen*, the court reasoned that a separate covenant is implied between the seller and purchaser: "because of the unusual dependent relationship of the vendee to the vendor." *Id.* at 1158.

10.   For the court to have found for the plaintiffs in *Kelley*, the plaintiffs would have had to establish:

(1)   the condominium conversion required "extensive rehabilitative construction";

(2)   the defects complained of by the condominium owners were defects of the "new"

construction; and

(3)   the defects complained of were "latent" defects. *Kelley*, 478 N.E.2d at 1349.

✦EXERCISE 27.U - APOSTROPHE

This exercise should be done after reading Section 27.4 in the *Handbook*.

✦Form the possessive of the underlined nouns.

1. <u>judge</u> error

2. <u>judges</u> errors

3. <u>prosecuting attorney</u> assistant

4. <u>son-in-law</u> employer

5. <u>it</u>

6. <u>Terry and Howard</u> children (joint possession)

7. <u>Terry and Howard</u> children (individual possession)

8. <u>Lois</u> complaint

9. <u>fringe benefits</u> value

10. <u>two weeks</u> vacation

✦EXERCISE 27.V - APOSTROPHE

This exercise should be done after reading Section 27.4 in the *Handbook*.

◆Form the plural possessive of each of the following words.

1. agency

2. Mathews

3. security

4. Davis

5. bar examiner

◆EXERCISE 27.W - APOSTROPHE

This exercise should be done after reading Section 27.4 in the *Handbook*.

◆Use apostrophes to form the possessive, the plural, or the plural possessive, as indicated, of the underlined words.

1. 100 (form plural)

2. prostitute clientele (form plural possessive)

3. electrician union (form plural possessive)

4. franchise securities (form singular possessive)

5. Doris and Thomas executors (individual possession)

6. for old times sake (form possessive)

7. change the Mary to *Mari* (form the plural)

8. promissory note validity (form singular possessive)

9. policy effects (form plural possessive)

10. tenant organization (form plural possessive)

11. Schultz automobile (form singular possessive)

12. Schultz automobile (form plural possessive)

13. boss meeting (form plural possessive)

14. the Mayor of New York statement (form possessive)

15. Clinton & Nelson construction company (form joint possessive)

16. 1980 (form plural)

17. justice of the peace decision (form possessive)

18. too many if (form plural)

19. somebody else problem (form possessive)

20. who (form possessive)

✦EXERCISE 27.X - OTHER PUNCTUATION

This exercise should be done after reading Section 27.5 in the *Handbook*.

✦Find and correct the errors in quotation marks, ellipses, brackets, and parentheses in the following sentences. If there are no errors, simply mark the sentence as correct.

1. The word "aid" means all assistance whether given by words, acts, encouragement, support, or presence.

2. The hearing examiner found the zoning code to be slightly ambiguous:

    It is clear that this controversy could have been avoided if the Zoning code definition presented more specific information as to whether the fee underlying a street should be included in lot area calculations.

    CP. 60-61.

3. A "lot" is defined as follows:

> a platted or unplatted parcel of land unoccupied, occupied or to be occupied by a
> principal use or building and accessory buildings, together with such yards and
> open spaces as are required by this subtitle and <u>abutting by not less than twenty</u>
> <u>feet upon a street</u> sufficiently improved for automotive travel or having an
> exclusive, unobstructed permanent access easement serving not more than two
> principal uses and jointly owned by the two property owners served and at least
> twenty feet wide and not exceeding one hundred fifty feet in length to such street.
> (Emphasis added.) Denver Mun. Code §24.08.130(3).

4. Summary judgment ". . . shall be rendered forthwith if the pleadings, depositions,
answers to interrogatories, and admissions on file, together with the affidavits, if any,
show that there is no genuine issue as to any material fact and that the moving party is
entitled to a judgment as a matter of law." Fed. R. Civ. P. 56(c).

5. Wilson claims that one of the photographs admitted into evidence depicts him in a " . . .
vampire-like . . ." pose.

6. As noted in *Coolidge*, the scope of a search is limited, and officers must have justification
for being in a position to view the incriminating evidence:

> "[I]t is important to keep in mind that, in the vast majority of cases, any evidence
> seized by the police will be in plain view, at least at the moment of seizure. The

194

problem with the 'plain view' doctrine has been to identify the circumstances in which plain view has legal significance rather than being simply the normal concomitant of any search, legal or illegal."

403 U.S. at 465.

7.   Using the standard enunciated in *Berenson*, the *Kurzius* court held that "A zoning ordinance will be invalidated on both constitutional and state statutory grounds if it was enacted with an exclusionary purpose, or it ignores regional needs and has an unjustifiably exclusionary effect." *Id.* at 343, 414 N.E.2d at 682.

8.   The federal courts have frequently been at odds concerning whether a particular offense constitutes a crime of " . . .   deceit or false statement."

9.   The trial court did not err in failing to define "unlawful act".

10.   In *Texas v. Brown*, the United States Supreme Court described the standard of probable cause as it relates to the plain view doctrine:

> "As the court frequently has remarked, probable cause is a flexible, common sense standard. It merely requires that the facts available to the officer would 'warrant a man of reasonable caution in the belief,' *Carrol v. United States*, 267 U.S. 132, 162 (1925), that certain items may be . . . useful as evidence of a crime; it does not demand any showing that such a belief be correct or more likely true than false.

A 'practical, nontechnical probability' that incriminating evidence is involved is all that is required."

Texas v. Brown, 460 U.S. at 742.

✦EXERCISE 27.Y   HYPHENS

This exercise should be done after reading Section 27.5.5 in the *Handbook.*

✦Add hyphens to the following phrases as needed.

1. posthumous work

2. non stock corporation

3. multinational corporation

4. six month lease

5. poorly reasoned opinion

6. ex husband

7. extremely volatile solution

8. all inclusive report

9. ex parte proceeding

10. fact finding commission

11. priest penitent privilege

12. low to moderate-income housing

✦EXERCISE 27.Z HYPHENS

This exercise should be done after reading Section 27.5.5 in the *Handbook*.

✦Decide which of the following sentences have the hyphen used correctly.

1. Hanson's case falls within an area of law that is well settled.

2. Hanson's case falls within a well-settled area of law.

3. Common law is all the statutory and case law of England and the American colonies before the American revolution.

4. The court recognized the couple's common law marriage.

5. The defendant has held two prominent position in the community: Chief of Police and Editor-in-Chief of the local newspaper.

6. The State has Howard's taped statement, which could be used on cross examination.

7. The trial court relied on the higher "substantial evidence" test and weighed the evidence of duress, thereby usurping the fact-finding function of the jury.

8. It is well-settled that the scope of a protective order limiting discovery or disclosure at trial is within the broad discretion of the trial court. *See Rhinehart v. Seattle Times, Inc.,* 98 Wash. 2d 226, 654 P.2d 673 (1982*); Penberthy Electromelt Int'l v. United States Gypsum Co.,* 38 Wash. App. 514, 686 P.2d 1138 (1984).

9. Meyers's case falls within a well settled area of law and raises no issues deserving this court's immediate attention.

10. In a series of post-trial motions, Rudolph renewed his constitutional claims and requested a new trial based upon the ability of Carter to testify.

✦EXERCISE 27.AA - COMMA SPLICES AND FUSED SENTENCES

✦Read the following sentences and first determine if the sentence contains a comma spice or if the sentence is a fused sentence. If the sentence has either problem, rewrite the sentence, correcting the problem.

1. Our clients, the Kearneys, were served with a complaint by their neighbor, Mr. Bob Cratchett, who asks the court to eject the Kearneys from a ten-foot strip of land between the property of the two neighbors.

2. Mr. Cratchett bought the property sometime in 1988, the facts are in dispute as to the specific month.

3. Before Mr. Cratchett bought the property, it was owned by Mrs. Moriarty she died in October 1987.

4. Since 1976, the Kearneys have used the property in a variety of ways, for example, they have regularly mowed the grass in the disputed area since 1976 or 1977.

5. The Kearneys have maintained the picnic area over the years and have used it almost daily during the summer months.

6. During the time period from 1977 to 1978, they ejected any trespassers when those trespassers tried to use the picnic area.

7. When the Kearneys built the patio area, they did not ask Mrs. Moriarty for permission, Mrs. Moriarty did not object to their use of the area before or after the patio was built.

8. Mrs. Moriarty, however, used the picnic area for her own family picnics, although not as frequently as the Kearneys.

9. The Kearneys did not get along with Mr. Cratchett in the way they did with Mrs. Moriarty because he had loud parties and because he let his dogs run free.

10. Mr. Cratchett believed that the boundary line between the two properties was the retaining wall that had been mistakenly extended onto Mr. Moriarty's property, however, in October 1989, he had his land surveyed and learned the of true property line.

✦EXERCISE 27.BB - COMMA SPLICES AND FUSED SENTENCES

✦Read the following paragraphs and correct all comma splices and fused sentences.

Alaska Statute §09.10.030 and the Alaska common law govern the Kearneys claim to quiet title for the disputed strip of land under the doctrine of adverse possession. The court will award the Kearneys title to the land if they can show that their use and possession of the land was continuous for the statutory period, open and notorious, and exclusive and hostile to the record owner.

It is undisputed that the Kearneys have possessed the disputed strip of land for over ten years, however, a problem exists in proving the continuous element because we must also show that the record owner has at no time interrupted the Kearneys' possession of the land. While Mrs. Kearney was alive, she used the land in conjunction with the Kearneys, as a result, this element will have to be decided by a jury.

The second element should be easily satisfied by the Kearneys' improvements to and maintenance of the disputed strip of land. In addition, the Kearneys' use of the land demonstrates that they provided notice to the record holder of their adverse claim.

The Kearneys can satisfy the first half of the third element, exclusive use, by showing that they acted to exclude all other people from the land, although they did allow Mrs. Morarity to use the land while she was alive. Consequently, the first half of this element will have to be decided by a jury.

The Kearneys will argue that they satisfy the second half of the third element, hostile possession, they will show that they acted as any true owner would be maintaining and improving the land. These acts put Mrs. Morarity on notice of the adverse claim they show that she acquiesced to the Kearneys' use. These facts will be disputed, however, because Mr. Cratchett will claim that Mrs. Morarity merely gave the Kearneys permission to use her land and as a result, this half of the third element will also have to be decided by a jury.

USAGE

◆From the choices in parentheses, choose the word that is better or correct usage for legal writing.

1. No evidence exists from which the jury could (infer/imply) that Dotson committed the lesser crime of possessing a controlled substance.

2. Instruction 22 makes a (principal/principle) liable through the acts of an agent if the (principal/principle) intentionally directed, authorized, encouraged, or consented to the unlawful acts.

3. All six elements of the crime cannot possibly be (proved/proven) beyond a reasonable doubt.

4. (When/where) the injury to the land is temporary and the land can be restored to (it's/its) original condition, the measure is the cost of restoration plus the diminished use value of the property during restoration.

5. (Because/since) you made the improvements to the land, you have treated the section between the two fences as your own.

Answers
Writing Exercises
◆◆◆

✦EXERCISE 21.A - PARAGRAPH LENGTH

Although the original author of this paragraph did in fact write it as one paragraph, most readers would agree that even with the frequent signposts ("the first exception," "in the instant case," "the second exception," and "in the instant case") this paragraph is too long for readers to assimilate comfortably.

There are a number of ways to break this selection into shorter paragraphs, including the two that follow.

✦Option 1

There are some limited exceptions to the prohibitive rule stated in the above cases; however, the facts of the instant case do not fall into those exceptions.

The first exception allows the questioning of a witness about religious beliefs when those beliefs are relevant to some issue other than the credibility of the witness. *State v. Stone*, 728 P.2d 674 (Ariz. Ct. App. 1986). In the instant case, Ms. Patten's religious activities and beliefs were not at issue and the only conceivable purpose that the prosecution could have had for questioning her about them was to bolster her credibility by impressing the jury with her religiousness.

The second exception applies when reference to the religious beliefs of a witness is isolated and not significant to the trial proceedings in their entirety. *Id.* at 871, 728 P.2d at 678. In the instant case, the prosecution's questions--over repeated objections--about Ms. Patten's religious beliefs, as well as the closing argument comments about those beliefs, cannot be deemed isolated and inadvertent. (RP 151-52, 186).

Under the third exception, inquiry about the religious beliefs of a witness will not give rise to constitutional error if the assigning party invites the error. *People v. Baseer*, 90 Ill. App. 3d 866, 414 N.E.2d 5 (1980). Hence, when a defendant testifies as to his own religious beliefs in an attempt to bolster his credibility, he will not be heard to complain when the prosecution cross-examines him about his beliefs. *Id.* at 871, 414 N.E.2d at 10. In the instant case, Mr. Davidson's counsel never attempted to question Ms. Patten about her religious beliefs so as to affect her credibility, so it cannot be said that the defense "opened the door" to the prosecution's questioning of Ms. Patten about her religious beliefs. *Id.*

In short, none of the exceptions apply. Therefore, the trial court's allowance of the prosecution's questioning was an error of constitutional magnitude.

✦Option 2
(Same as Option 1 except paragraphs 1 and 2 are combined)

There are some limited exceptions to the prohibitive rule stated in the above cases; however, the facts of the instant case do not fall into those exceptions. The first exception allows the questioning of a witness about religious beliefs when those beliefs are relevant to some issue other than the credibility of the witness. *State v. Stone*, 728 P.2d 674 (Ariz. Ct. App. 1986). In the instant case, Ms. Patten's religious activities and beliefs were not at issue and the only conceivable purpose that the prosecution could have had for questioning her about them was to bolster her credibility by impressing the jury with her religiousness.

The second exception applies when reference to the religious beliefs of a witness is isolated and not significant to the trial proceedings in their entirety. *Id.* at 871, 728 P.2d at 678. In the instant case, the prosecution's questions--over repeated objections-- about Ms. Patten's religious beliefs, as well as the closing argument comments about those beliefs, cannot be deemed isolated and inadvertent. (RP 151-52, 186).

Under the third exception, inquiry about the religious beliefs of a witness will not give rise to constitutional error if the assigning party invites the error. *People v. Baseer*, 90 Ill. App. 3d 866, 414 N.E.2d 5 (1980). Hence, when a defendant testifies as to his own religious beliefs in an attempt to bolster his credibility, he will not be heard to complain when the prosecution cross-examines him about his beliefs. *Id.* at 871, 414 N.E.2d at 10. In the instant case, Mr. Davidson's counsel never attempted to question Ms. Patten about her religious beliefs so as to affect her credibility, so it cannot be said that the defense "opened the door" to the prosecution's questioning of Ms. Patten about her religious beliefs. *Id.*

In short, none of the exceptions apply. Therefore, the trial court's allowance of the prosecution's questioning was an error of constitutional magnitude.

✦EXERCISE 21.B - PARAGRAPH LENGTH

Paragraph 1 would work better if divided into two paragraphs. Divide between the second and third sentences. The first two sentences provide background information. The next three sentences focus on the complaint and possible remedies.

Although the paragraph about Mr. Baker is a one-sentence paragraph, it works well because the writer has chosen to use a separate paragraph to describe each plaintiff's complaints.

The one-sentence paragraph at the end of the statement of facts, however, is ineffective. Obviously, the writer had one additional significant fact but did not know where to put it. Because it is a background fact, it is probably best to work it into the opening paragraph, which includes other background facts.

Possible Revision of opening paragraph:

Despite several neighbors' complaints, the Metropolitan School Board has allowed Say No to Drugs (SND) baseball games to be played at Urban High on Tuesday and Thursday from 8 p.m. to midnight. The School Board has supported the SND program because it is a successful, nationally recognized program aimed at local drug users and because Urban High's field is the only lighted baseball field within a ten-mile radius of Urban High.

✦EXERCISE 21.C - TOPIC SENTENCES

1. The topic sentence in the original is "Even though the more current cases adopt a liberal reading, there are cases that support a motion to quash service." Presumably, the opening clause is a transition from the preceding discussion. The main clause, "there are cases that support a motion to quash service," is weak. All it says are that the cases exist; it does not get to the real point, which is in the next sentence.

   Possible revision: Even though the more current cases adopt a liberal reading, cases that support a motion to quash service limit *Rovinski* by recognizing that it is not enough to have actual notice.

2. The original topic sentence in this paragraph is "In order to use *Frasca* to support our

client, we must characterize Ms. Clay-Poole's trips to California as visits." The writer may have correctly stated the point of the paragraph in the topic sentence -- the trips to California must be characterized as visits -- but she has written a rather weak transition.

Possible revision: Like Frasca's visits to Pennsylvania, Ms. Clay-Poole's trips to

California were also visits.

If the real point of the paragraph was that her contacts with the California house were minimal, then the topic sentence should state that point.

Possible revision: Like the defendant in *Frasca*, Ms. Clay-Poole can argue that her

contacts with the California residence were minimal.

3.   The topic sentence --the plaintiff will point out the factual differences between our case and *Frasca* -- does introduce the paragraph, but that is about it. All it does is state the obvious. The sentence lacks both a transition and a general statement about the point of the

Possible revision: The plaintiff, on the other hand, will try to distinguish *Frasca* by

showing that Clay-Poole's contacts with the California house are more extensive than

Frasca's contacts with the Pennsylvania house.

4.   The topic sentence -- Concerning element number one, was Smith a member of the ADEA protected class at the time of his discharge? -- is awkward and unsophisticated. Besides beginning with a dangling modifier, "Concerning element number one," it wastes time by asking an obvious question. Avoid such rhetorical questions in memo writing. A better revision is to begin with the answer to that question.

Possible revision: Smith satisfies element number one because he was a member of the

ADEA protected class. At the time of Smith's discharge, ADEA applied only to

individuals who were at least forty years old but less than seventy years old. 29 U.S.C.

§631(a)(1982). Smith was forty-nine years old when he was discharged; therefore, he

211

was within the ADEA protected class.

✦Exercise 21.D - Topic and Concluding Sentences

The topic sentence is effective because it tells the reader why *Riblet v. Spokane-Portland Cement Co.* is begin discussed. Notice how the topic sentence is a generalization which is then supported by the specific facts of the case. The conclusion is effective because it brings the reader back to the topic sentence generalization -- damages for annoyances -- but now the discussion has advanced so that the reader knows which annoyances are compensable.

✦Exercise 21.E - Paragraph Blocks

Topic Paragraph	=	"Actual physical control" . . . public."
Topic Sentence	=	Considering the fact pattern . . . discussion."
Topic Sentence	=	"Although the primary issue . . . analysis."
(introduces paragraph block)		
Topic Sentence	=	"In fact, . . . decision."
Topic Paragraph	=	"Although it is . . . (1958)."
Topic Sentence	=	"The elements . . . some clarification."
Topic Sentence	=	"The Montana court . . . roadway."
Topic Sentence	=	"The Renko fact pattern . . . roadway."
Topic Sentence	=	"Positioning . . . flow of traffic)."
Topic Sentence	=	"The Montana court . . . dissenting)."
Topic Sentence	=	"Because only . . . legal significance."
Topic Sentence	=	"In contrast . . . turned off."
Topic Sentence	=	"In short, . . . to sleep."
Topic Sentence	=	"With regard . . . apparatus."

Topic Sentence	=	"As a sub-issue . . . required."
Topic Sentence	=	"If some form . . . (1984."
Topic Sentence	=	"The second question, . . . intent."
		"Intent . . . two ways."
Topic Sentence	=	"Recent statutory . . . reasoning."
Topic Sentence	=	"It does not matter . . . seat."
Topic Sentence	=	"The Montana court . . . intoxicated."

(introduces paragraph block)

Topic Sentence	=	"Focusing . . . accidents."

Note that short paragraph blocks (for example, only two paragraphs) are often introduced by just a topic sentence, not a full topic paragraph.

Note that on at least one occasion, two sentences work together to create a "topic sentence."

Notice too that this example shows a <u>nesting</u> of paragraph blocks within paragraph blocks. The first paragraph after the heading "Actual Physical Control" is a topic paragraph for the rest of the discussion section, which is one very large paragraph block. Within the very large block is a large paragraph block that begins with the paragraph "The Renko fact pattern differs in the following respects . . . " and includes the rest of the paragraphs in the discussion section. And within the large paragraph block described in the preceding sentence, there is yet another smaller paragraph block starting with the paragraph "In short, . . ." and including the next four paragraphs!

To see the carefully crafted paragraph structure of the discussion section, then, review the following version, which has Roman numerals, capitals, numbers, and lowercase letters to show the nesting block effect.

<u>Discussion</u>

I.   "Actual physical control" is governed by a statute that states in part: "It is unlawful . . .

for any person who is under the influence of alcohol to . . . be in actual physical control of a motor vehicle upon the ways of this state open to the public." Mont. Code Ann. §61.8.4011(a)(1983). Generally, three elements of the statute bear examination: 1) the person must be under the influence of alcohol; 2)the person must be in actual physical control of a motor vehicle; and 3) the motor vehicle must be on the ways of Montana that are open to the public.

<u>Under the Influence</u>

A.   Considering the fact pattern of the Renko case, the court will probably find that the question of whether Mr. Renko was under the influence of alcohol is not worthy of in-depth discussion. The results of the breathalyzer test, the vomit, and the testimony of the arresting officer establish that our client was legally intoxicated at the time of arrest, so the first element of the offense is not at issue.

<u>Ways of the State</u>

B.   Although the primary issue of the case focuses upon resolving questions pertaining to actual physical control, the issue of whether Mr. Renko's truck was on the ways of the state open to the public deserves brief analysis. The traffic code states that "'ways of the state open to the public' means any highway, road, alley lane, parking area, or other public or private place adapted and fitted for public travel that is in common use by the public." Mont. Code Ann. §61.8.101(1)(1983). The language specifically states "adapted and fitted for

214

public travel." Since Mr. Renko's truck was found on the shoulder, the court

would have to determine whether the shoulder of a highway is adapted and fitted

for public travel. In defining other statutory language, the Montana Supreme

Court resorted to dictionary definitions. Webster defines shoulder as "either edge

of a roadway; specifically: the part of the roadway *outside the traveled way*"

(emphasis added). It is possible, then, that the court could interpret the statutory

language narrowly and conclude that the term "ways" does not encompass

shoulders.

However, a narrow construction of the term "ways" is unlikely. In fact, there are two

strong indications that Montana will favor a broad construction: 1) an extension stated in the

statutory definition of "highway"; and 2) an interpretation of "ways" given in a Montana

Supreme Court decision. By statutory definition, "[h]ighway means the entire width between the

boundary lines of every publicly maintained way when any part thereof is open to the use of the

public for purposes of vehicular travel, *except that for the purpose of chapter 8 the term also*

includes ways which have been or shall be dedicated to public use." (emphasis added) Mont.

Code Ann. §61.1.201 (1983). Chapter 8 includes offenses committed while under the influence

of alcohol. Since the legislature expanded the statutory definition for alcohol-related offenses, it

follows that the legislature intended to broaden, not narrow, the term. Following the legislature's

lead, the Montana Supreme Court stipulated that "ways" encompasses state and county right-of-

ways, including borrow pits, which road maintenance crews use as sources of dirt and gravel.

State v. Taylor, 242 Mont. 43, 44, 661 P.2d 33, 34 (1983). It is highly unlikely that the court

215

would include borrow pits but exempt shoulders from the term "ways." The court will probably conclude that Mr. Renko's truck was on the ways of the state open to the public.

Actual Physical Control

C.   Although it is relatively easy to determine that the facts in this case satisfy the elements of "under the influence" and "on the ways," it is more difficult to decide whether they constitute "actual physical control" of a motor vehicle. The statute does not further explain "actual physical control," but the Montana Supreme Court supplied the following dictionary definition: "[I]t means existing or present bodily restraint, directing influence, domination or regulation of an automobile." *State v. Ruona*, 133 Mont. 243, 246, 321 P.2d 615, 618 (1958).

The elements of the definition have not been completely defined; however, the court has given some clarification. In *Ruona*, the court stated that "restraint" includes preventing a car from moving; movement of a vehicle is not necessary for actual physical control. 133 Mont. at 246, 321 P.2d at 618. The court further clarified the term "regulation" by asserting that a sleeping driver who remains behind the steering wheel of a vehicle "remains in a position to regulate" the vehicle and "has not relinquished control" of the vehicle. *Taylor*, 242 Mont. at 44, 661 P.2d 34. Regulation or control is not diminished by the fact that a vehicle is incapable of moving because, as previously noted, movement is not required. *Taylor*, 242 Mont. at 44, 661 P.2d at 34 (citing *Ruona*, 133 Mont. at 247, 321 P.2d at 619).

216

The Montana court has applied these definitions to cases with the following fact patterns: 1) the driver was asleep and intoxicated; 2) the driver was positioned behind the steering wheel of the motor vehicle; 3) the vehicle's motor was running; 4) the vehicle was parked; and 5) the vehicle was at least partially on the pavement of a roadway. In both of the leading Montana cases, the court held that the driver was in actual physical control of his vehicle. *Ruona*, 133 Mont. 243, 321 P.2d 615; *Taylor*, 242 Mont. 43, 661 P.2d 33. However, the court has not addressed the exact fact pattern presented by the Renko case.

The Renko fact pattern differs in the following respects: 1) the driver was not seated behind the steering wheel; 2) the engine of the vehicle was not running; and 3) the vehicle was not even partially on the traveled portion of the roadway. Although the "driver's position" may be considered separately, "engine not running" and "vehicle not on roadway" are closely related in terms of legal significance and should be analyzed together. In fact, the interrelationship of all three factors should be considered for two reasons. First, although a single factor may not affect the outcome of a case, the combination of that factor with others may be legally significant. Second, the combination of the aforementioned factors may be important in showing the defendant's intent.

1. Positioning in the driver's seat is a common element in all the national cases that have found actual physical control of a motionless vehicle, *State v. Smelter*, 36 Wash. App. 439, 441, 674 P.2d 690, 692 (1984), except for one Oklahoma case, *Hughes v. State*, 509 Okla., 157, 535 P.2d 1023

217

(1975) (Defendant was lying across the front seat but was awake and the vehicle was not only on the roadway but also at a 90 degree angle to the flow of traffic.) The theory behind the decisions is that an intoxicated person who is seated behind the steering wheel is still in a position to control the vehicle and could be considered a potential threat to the public. *Ruona*, 133 Mont. at 243, 321 P.2d at 619 (quoting *State v. Webb*, 78 Ariz. 8, 274 P.2d 338, (1954)).

The Montana court could view the positioning question in two ways: 1) it could hold that positioning behind the steering wheel is essential to manifest control of the vehicle, *Cincinnati v. Kelley*, 47 Ohio St. 2d 94, 351 N.E.2d 85 (1976); or 2) it could find that positioning is relatively unimportant because once awakened, a driver could quickly move behind the wheel and would pose as great a threat to society as the driver who remained behind the wheel while he slept. *State v. Bugger,* 25 Utah 2d 404, 483 P.2d 442, (1971) (Ellett, J., dissenting). Considering that the Montana court has focused on the idea that the purpose of the statute is to protect the public and has found that a sleeping, intoxicated driver is still a threat to the public, *Ruona*, 133 Mont. at 243, 321 P.2d at 619, the court would probably find that a sleeping, intoxicated driver who is lying on the front seat poses a potential threat to the public.

2. Because only a few cases have addressed the issues of whether actual physical control of a vehicle can be established when the engine is not running or when the vehicle is entirely off the traveled portion of the

218

roadway, it is difficult to isolate these factors in terms of legal significance.

Actual physical control has been found when the vehicle was legally parked and the engine was not running but when the driver was awake and in the driver's seat. *Kelley*, 47 Ohio St. 2d 94, 351 N.E.2d 85. In *Kelley*, the court noted that the defendant was behind the wheel, had possession of the key, and was in such a condition that he could have started the vehicle. 47 Ohio St. 2d 94, 351 N.E.2d 85.

In contrast, courts have been reluctant to find actual physical control when the driver has been found asleep in a vehicle that was legally parked on the shoulder of the roadway with the engine turned off. For example, in *State v. Bugger*, the Utah Supreme Court held that a defendant was not in actual physical control because he was not controlling the vehicle or exercising any dominion over it. *State v. Bugger*, 25 Utah 2d 404, 483 P.2d 442. In *State v. Zavala*, the Arizona Supreme Court held that a defendant had voluntarily relinquished control of the vehicle. *State v. Zavala*, 136 Ariz. 356, 666 P.2d 456 (1983). The Arizona court considered the voluntary action or intent of the driver important and wished to foster the policy of encouraging drunk drivers to pull out of traffic, to turn off the engine, and to go to sleep. *Zavala*, 136 Ariz. 356, 666 P.2d 456 (1983).

In short, before the Montana court can determine whether Mr. Renko was in actual physical control of the vehicle, the court must determine the following issues: 1) whether Mr. Renko had relinquished control of the vehicle; and 2) whether the Montana legislature intended

219

to foster a policy of encouraging intoxicated drivers to pull off the road to sleep.

a.　With regard to the first issue, other jurisdictions have partially defined "control" and "operate" in terms of the defendant's manipulation of mechanical or electrical apparatus. Cases that relate to such a definition have dealt with defendants who were awake and were attempting either to brake or to steer inoperable vehicles. *State v. Swift*, 125 Conn. 399, 6 A.2d 359 (1939); *State v. Storrs*, 105 Vt. 180, 163 A. 56 (1933). However, it is conceivable that a court, particularly one that is inclined to broadly construe traffic regulations concerning intoxicated drivers, could apply the "manipulation of mechanical and electrical apparatus" definition in the Renko case. The court could conclude that Mr. Renko's left foot was manipulating the brake pedal and illuminating the brake lights; therefore, he had not relinquished control of the vehicle. The court could reach the same conclusion by finding that Mr. Renko was using "present bodily restraint" to prevent the car from moving.

As a subissue in determining control, the court would have to address the question of whether operability is required. If it is not required, then no further discussion of this issue would be necessary; and in light of the Montana court's holding in *Taylor*, operability probably would not be required because movement is not required and the driver was still considered to be in actual physical control of a vehicle that he could not move. 242 Mont. at 43, 661 P.2d at 34.

If some form of operability is required, then the court must decide whether to focus on the defendant's ability to operate the vehicle or on the vehicle's condition. *State v. Smelter*, 36 Wash. App. 439, 444, 674 P.2d 690, 693 (1984). In focusing on the defendant's condition, the court could find that since the defendant had the key and was in the cab of the truck, he would have been able to operate the vehicle had he been awakened. Not only is it possible that he could have operated the truck, it is evident that he did drive the truck from the tavern to the freeway before parking it on the shoulder. In focusing on the vehicle's condition, the Washington court used the trial court's "reasonably operable" standard and defined that term as any malfunction short of a cracked block or a similar problem that would render the vehicle totally inoperable. *Smelter*, 36 Wash. App. at 444, 674 P.2d at 693. By that definition, Mr. Renko's truck was reasonably operable regardless of whether it would start. Therefore, if the Montana court considers operability an issue, it would probably find that Mr. Renko was capable of operating the vehicle and that the vehicle was in reasonably operable condition.

b.   The second question, whether the legislature wishes to foster a policy of encouraging intoxicated drivers to pull off the road to sleep, includes considering the importance of the defendant's intent. Intent and policy an be looked at in two ways. The first, that presented by the Arizona court in *Zavala*, is that the driver

221

who realizes that he is not in condition to drive and pulls off the roadway to sleep should be rewarded. If the court were not to reward such behavior, then the driver would be tempted to proceed to his destination and would present a greater threat to public safety. 136 Ariz. 356, 666 P.2d 456. The second view is that the drunken driver not only intended to drive but also did drive his car from the tavern to the freeway, and it is better policy to encourage an intoxicated person to avoid driving in the first place. In accord with this view, the Washington court noted that statutes prohibiting driving while intoxicated are primarily preventive measures that are designed to deter intoxicated persons from entering vehicles except as passengers. *Smelter*, 36 Wash. App. at 444, 674 P.2d at 693 (citing *State v. Ghylin*, 250 N.W.2d 252, 255 (N.D. 1977)). The *Smelter* court agreed with other courts that have held that such legislation should be liberally interpreted with the effect of promoting the public interest at the expense of the private interest of the inebriated driver. 36 Wash. App. at 444, 674 P.2d at 693.

Recent statutory revisions in Montana seem to follow this line of reasoning. The Montana legislature revised the traffic code in 1983 and purposely broadened the scope of the laws relating to drunken drivers. The intent was to allow patrol officers to apprehend drunken drivers before such drivers could create accidents. *Montana's Legislative Attempt to Deal with the Drinking Driver: The 1983 DWI Statutes*, 46 Mont. L. Rev. 315 (1985). The Montana court followed suit in *Taylor* by liberally construing the statutes. 242 Mont. 43, 661 P.2d 33. Considering the legislative intent and the court's demonstrated tendencies toward liberal construction, the court will probably side with Justice Ellett, who dissented in *Bugger:*

It does not matter whether the motor is running or is idle nor whether the drunk is in the front seat or in the back seat. His potentiality for harm is lessened but not obviated by a silent motor or a backseat position--provided, of course, that he is the one in control of the car. It only takes a flick of the wrist to start the motor or to engage the gears, and it requires only a moment of time to get under the wheel from the back seat. A drunk in control of a motor vehicle has such a propensity to cause harm that the statute intended to make it criminal for him to be in a position to do so. *State v. Bugger*, 25 Utah 2d 404, 405, 483 P.2d 442, 443 (1971) (Ellett, J., dissenting).

Conclusion

II.   The Montana court will probably find that Andrew Renko was in actual physical control of a motor vehicle while intoxicated. Although it would be unprecedented to find "actual physical control" when the person was asleep across the front seat and the engine was not running, the Montana court has not been reluctant to break new ground. The court was a leader in defining "actual physical control," and many jurisdictions have followed the Montana definition.

Focusing on the threat to the public, the Montana legislature broadened the statutes to make it easier to apprehend intoxicated individuals before they cause motor vehicle accidents. The Montana court followed suit by broadly construing statutory wording. The tendency in Montana is toward an expanded definition. Therefore, it would be inconsistent for the court to conclude that Mr. Renko was not in actual physical control of his vehicle.

✦EXERCISE 21.F - PARAGRAPH BLOCKS

Concluding Sentence	=	"The results . . . not at issue."
Concluding Sentence	=	"It is possible . . . shoulders."
Concluding Sentence	=	"The court will . . . public."
(for paragraph block)		
Concluding Sentence	=	"The statute . . . (1958)."
Concluding Sentence	=	"Regulation . . . at 619."
Concluding Sentence	=	"However, . . . Renko case."
Concluding Sentence	=	"In fact, . . . reasons."
Concluding Sentence	=	"The theory . . . 1954)."
		"First . . . Second . . . intent"
Concluding Sentence	=	"Considering . . . to the public."
Concluding Sentence	=	"The court could conclude . . . The court could reach . . . morning"
Concluding Sentence	=	"If it is not . . . at 34."

Concluding Sentence	=	"Therefore, . . . operable condition."
Concluding Sentence	=	"The *Smelter* court . . . at 693."
Concluding Sentence	=	"Considering . . . in *Bugger*."
Concluding Paragraph	=	"It does not matter . . . dissenting."
Concluding Sentence	=	"The court was a leader . . . definition."
Concluding Sentence	=	"Therefore, . . . vehicle."

Note that many paragraphs do not have explicit concluding sentences.

✦EXERCISE 21.G - PARAGRAPH LENGTH

Different readers will have different opinions about whether the paragraphs are too long or too short in the example. Most readers find the one-sentence paragraph ("In short, . . .) effective because it introduces a paragraph block and even though it is only one sentence, it is a rather long sentence with two distinct parts.

Chapter 22
Connections Between Sentences

◆**EXERCISE 22.A GENERIC TRANSITIONS**

1.   for one year. Recently, Mr. Hillary has been annoyed   . . . .

2.   requirements. Therefore, he OR requirements; therefore,

3.   Hillary will further (also) claim that he is specially injured . . . .

4.   (1964). Consequently, the fact that . . . .

5.   (1956). Moreover, the use . . . .

6.   (1930). Similarly, Hillary . . . .

7.   subjective values. Rather, the presence of

8.   public nuisance. He could, however, consider . . . .

9.   compelling. First, the noise . . . "ordinary." *Hayes*, 311. Second, it . . . manner." *Id.*
      Third, no intoxicants . . . beach. *Id.* at 313. Fourth, the activities . . . .

10.   recreation. In addition, the court found . . . .

◆**EXERCISE 22. B DOVETAILING**

1.   For this information, the Justice Department offered him a reward.

2.   His only motive for assisting the Justice Department was to receive a reward.

3.   These actions (or These operational actions) do not include discretionary, planning, or
      design actions.

4.   These acts are performed by agents who do not exercise their own judgment. OR The
      agents perform these acts without exercising their own judgment.

5. Because of these records, the IRS examined Mr. Snowadzki's tax returns . . . . OR
    These records prompted the IRS to examine . . . .

6. This legislation extended law enforcement jurisdiction and provided for faster and stiffer penalties.

7. The definition does not specifically address the shoulder of the highway.

8. In that decision, the court interpreted the statutory definition of highway to include the borrow pit.

9. Without any supporting authority, the court probably will not consider the position of Mr. Renko's head or body to be a significant factor.

10. This doctrine was adopted to compensate victims who had been injured by the negligent driving of minors.

✦EXERCISE 22.C DOVETAILING

1. The impact of the cars threw Mrs. White against . . . .
    As a result of the accident, Mrs. White gave birth . . . .
    Because of the loss of this child, Mrs. White is suffering
    . . . .

2. Such evidence might include injuries incurred by plaintiffs in similar situations. Using this evidence, a jury would determine . . . .

3. After conferring with panel members and considering their report, the Governor, by Executive Order, initiated a daycare facility program inspection . . . . The memorandum directed the inspectors to consider seven factors.

✦EXERCISE 22.D ALL TRANSITIONS

Mr. and Mrs. Abernathy, our clients, live in a mobile home park near <u>Vancouver, Washington. Because Vancouver</u> is located in Clark County, just across the Columbia River from Portland, Oregon. It is rapidly becoming a "bedroom community" for the <u>metropolitan Portland area</u>. (Note: the section of this sentence that is new information is "rapidly becoming a 'bedroom community." The word "Vancouver" is a sufficient dovetail to the previous sentence, so the writer can leave the other old information "metropolitan Portland area" at the end of the sentence.)

In 1979, Clark County enacted a mobile home park ordinance. The County passed the ordinance in response to the concerns of mobile home owners over the scarcity of mobile home spaces in the area and the tight restrictions on the use of rural land. Mobile home regulation is also covered by the Washington State Mobile Home Landlord-Tenant Act, passed by the legislature in 1977.

In October 1983, the Abernathys' landlord, Frank C. Johnson, informed them that, because of his increased operating expenses, he planned to raise their monthly rent from $275 to $500, effective January 1, 1984. The Abernathys' year-to-year lease expired at the time, and a renewal of the lease was contingent on their agreement to the rent increase.

On October 31, 1983, the Abernathys wrote to Mr. Johnson requesting arbitration as provided for in the county ordinance. The provision allows a mobile home owner presented with a lease or rental fee increase to petition for public factfinding by an arbitrator to determine whether the proposed rate is reasonable. Mr. Johnson did not respond to the Abernathys' request. (Note: here "the Abernathys' request" is old information and "did not respond" is the new information. The writer chose to disregard the old-new ideal pattern here to avoid a rather awkward passive construction "The Abernathys' request was not responded to by Mr. Johnson.")

On January 1, 1984, Mr. Johnson notified the Abernathys that they had failed to execute a lease. Therefore, they were to vacate the premises before February 29, 1984. The Abernathys refuse to leave.

Recently, Mr. Johnson filed an unlawful detainer action against the Abernathys. Among his claims is the assertion that the Clark County ordinance violates the taking provision of the Washington State and United States Constitution.

The Abernathys do not wish to vacate their trailer space. (Note: This entire sentence can probably be considered old information because the reader learned earlier that "The Abernathys refuse to leave." The sentence is not redundant, however, because it works with the rest of the concluding paragraph to establish the clients' current position.) They have asked whether the landlord acted properly when he raised their rent and when he sent them their termination notice. (Again, the underlined sections refer back to earlier points and adds the new information that they are asking if this is proper.) In addition, they want to know what rights and remedies they have under the state statute and the county ordinance. (Note: restructuring this sentence to move the old information before the new would yield a clumsy result.)

◆EXERCISE 22.E ALL TRANSITIONS

Any county, city, town, or
township may make and enforce
within its limits all such local

police, sanitary, and other regulations that do not conflict with general laws. Wash. Const. Art. 11, § 11 (1964). The power of a municipality to regulate a particular subject ceases when the state enacts a general law on that subject, unless there is room for concurrent jurisdiction. *Lenci v. City of end. Seattle*, 63 Wash. 2d 664, 669, 388, P.2d 926, 930 (1964). A municipality may enact local legislation upon subjects already covered by state legislation so long as its enactments do not conflict with the state legislation. *Id.* at 670, 388 P.2d at 931.

The old information "the power of a municipality to regulate a particular subject" has been moved to the front of the sentence; new information has been moved to the

Some shift of old information to beginning and new information to end of sentence.

Accordingly, the Washington Supreme Court has set out two tests to determine whether a local ordinance was "in conflict" with -- and therefore preempted by -- a state statute. First, if the state legislature's intent in enacting a statute was to completely occupy a given field of regulation, any local ordinance would be preempted by the statute, there being no room for concurrent jurisdiction. *Id.* at 669, 388 P.2d at 930. Second, if the express provisions of a local ordinance and of a state statute are in such direct conflict that they cannot be reconciled, the statute would prevail. *Id.* at 670, 388 P.2d at 931.

Change from a transition of contrast to one showing cause-effect relationship.

Generic transition to show sequence.
The "if" clause is a link back to two tests, so it should begin the sentence. The sentence now has a natural order of test, effect, reasoning.
Generic transition to show sequence.

230

In the case at hand, the Washington State Legislature had enacted a general law covering the regulation of mobile homes. Wash. Rev. Code § 519.20 (1977). If the legislature's intent in enacting the statute was to completely occupy the field, the Clark County Ordinance 79-801 covering the same subject would be preempted in its entirety.

Orienting transition added.

Old information shifted to beginning of sentence; new information shifted to the end.

Chapter 23
Effective Sentences

✦EXERCISE 23.A ACTIVE AND PASSIVE VOICE

1.   S = plaintiff V = accepted O = offer   ACTIVE

2.   S = (Texas) law V = requires O = balancing   ACTIVE

3.   S = term V = will be defined   PASSIVE

4.   S = court V = has followed   ACTIVE

5.   S = case V = may be strengthened   PASSIVE

6.   S = (prescriptive) easement V = had been established PASSIVE

7.   S = (objective) acts V = had established O = (prescriptive) easement   ACTIVE

8.   S = right V = can be revoked   PASSIVE

9.   S = Mrs. Townsend V = can revoke O = right   ACTIVE

10.   S = interpretation V = has been left   PASSIVE

This sentence is the most difficult in the exercise. It is passive voice because the interpretation is not doing the "has been left"; rather, "has been left" has been done to the interpretation. The real doer of the action "has been left" is hard to pinpoint because it is our system of laws and government that has us leave interpretation of rules up to the courts.

1.   Clyde Pearson <u>owns</u> Pearson & Sons Lawn Service.

2.   After Officer O'Neill <u>found</u> Mr. Lee's truck in the ditch, Officer O'Neill <u>called</u> for an ambulance.

3.   The Montana court <u>focused</u> on the idea that the legislature <u>intended</u> to prevent the dumping of toxic waste.

4.   Although the police <u>did not find</u> the marijuana in the bedroom, Officer Miller <u>found</u> a film canister filled with cocaine.

5.   The fourth amendment <u>stipulates</u> important particularities: the warrant <u>must state</u> the place to be searched and the things to be seized.

6.   The <u>Anderson</u> court's language <u>supports</u> Fremont's argument that the broad scope of the search <u>violated</u> his right to privacy.

7.   Apparently Tom <u>had driven</u> the business car on prior occasions, but his father <u>did not give</u> him specific permission to drive the business car on the day of the accident.

8.   The courts <u>have</u> not <u>ruled</u> on the question of whether a non-viable fetus is a minor child;

however, the courts <u>recognize</u> the rights of non-viable fetuses in other areas of the law.

9.   The Wilsons <u>should recover</u> the fair market value of the tractor because Washington tort law <u>provides</u> for the recovery of fair market value of property that has been destroyed.

10.   Statutory law <u>defines</u> private nuisance as "everything not included as a public nuisance."

✦EXERCISE 23.C   PASSIVE VOICE

1.   E   The person or thing performing the action is relatively unimportant.

2.   E   The subject "such arrangements" of the passive voice verb provides a strong link between the subordinate clause and the main clause.

3.   I   Active voice is more concise. Revise to "For the next ten years, all the landowners used the easement." (11 words in revision vs. 13 words in original)

            OR

      E   In a context in which the focus of the writing was on the easement itself and not the landowners who used it, then the original sentence would be effective.

4.   E   Passive voice in the clause allows the writer to place the connecting idea, the description of the assailant, at the end of the sentence where it can lead into the

subsequent sentence about the defendant's description. Passive voice is also more effective for the defendant because it downplays the doer of the action. Although a plaintiff's brief probably would not use the facts from these two sentences in this form, the active voice version-- "a white male with blue eyes and blond hair assaulted her"--would be more effective for the plaintiff.

5.   E   If the victim did not see her assailant, the person or thing performing the action is unknown. Again, the passive is more effective for the defendant.

OR

I   In a plaintiff's brief, the writer would want to use active voice and include the doer of the action if that person or thing is known: "Testimony from the attending physician corroborates the victim's testimony that the defendant struck her from behind."

6.   E   Passive voice in the first sentence moves the connecting idea, "Cathy Nock," to the end position. The second sentence begins with the connecting idea, "Ms. Nock."

7.   E   Person or thing performing the action is unknown or relatively unimportant.

8.   E   It is probably undesirable to disclose the identity of the person performing the action, or that person may be unknown. In a defendant's brief, the use of the

passive voice is more effective. In a plaintiff's brief the active voice would be more effective, particularly if the doer of the action is known.

9.   I   Active voice is more concise. Revise to "Both parties signed a standard form contract that detailed the terms of the agreement." (Fourteen words in revision vs. sixteen words in original.) Passive voice in original also separates subject from verb. (See Section D of this chapter.)

OR

E   However, in a context in which the focus of the writing is on the standard form contract, the passive voice may be more effective.

10.   E   Person or thing performing the action is relatively unimportant.

✦EXERCISE 23.D CONCRETE SUBJECTS

1.   S = It V = could be argued. Revision: The defense could argue that Mr. Smith was out of the state at the time of the robbery.

2.   S = It V = is. Revision: Both parties intended to enter into a contract. (Another possibility is to open the sentence with "clearly" as an emphasizer. However, many legal writers believe "clearly" is overused in legal writing and therefore ineffective.)

3.   S = It V = is. Revision: A fair market value probably does not exist for the poem.

4.   S = endorsement V = is required. The check must be endorsed before the funds can be

transferred.

OR The bank requires that the check be endorsed before the funds are transferred.

OR You must endorse the check before the funds can be transferred. Notice that you can

have a concrete subject with either an active or passive voice verb.

5.   S = It V = would appear. Revision: Apparently, our request will be granted.

OR Apparently, the court will grant our request. Notice that you can have a concrete

subject with either an active or passive voice verb.

6.   S = confirmation V = is required. Congress must confirm all federal judicial

appointments.

7.   S = It V = is. Revision: The defendant was refused admission to medical school because

of his criminal record.

8.   S = aspect V = is. Revision: Mr. Nolan's fingerprints on the knife will be difficult to

discount.

9.   S = It V = should be pointed out. Revision: South Land Timber's shipments to all three

customers were consistently late.

OR Add the person or thing doing the action "The prosecution should point out that

. . . ."

10.   S = factor V = caused. Revision: The defendant's earlier perjury conviction caused the

jury to discount her testimony in this case.

OR The jury discounted the defendant's testimony in this case because she had an earlier

perjury conviction.

✦EXERCISE 23.E ACTION VERBS

1.   S = way V = is. Revised: A court determines mutual assent by looking at the objective

manifestations of the parties' actions.

2.   S = governor V = made. Revised: The governor stated that he would not testify for the

defense.

3.   S = jury V = had. Revised: The jury knew about (of) the defendant's prior record.

4.   S = facts V = are. Revised: That witness must confirm several facts.

5.   S = <u>Hanford v. Goehry</u> V = concerned. Revised: In <u>Hanford v. Goehry</u>, a car was kept at the father's place of business.

6.   S = nurse V = made. Revised: The nurse attempted to disconnect the life support system.

7.   S = holding V = makes. Revised: The <u>Harbeson</u> court suggested that the Florida courts are moving towards compensation for loss without applying the old standards.

8.   S = instances V = were. Revised: The Parkers never asserted their rights against the Lindquists.

9.   S = <u>State v. Hughes</u> V = involved. Revised: In <u>State v. Hughes</u>, a defendant shot two police officers while resisting arrest for another murder.

10.   S = heirs V = are. Revised: The two heirs disagree over the division of property.

✦EXERCISE 23.F   SUBJECT-VERB DISTANCE

1.   S = contract V = was signed. Revised: Both parties signed a standard form contract that detailed all the terms of the agreement except for the shipper's liability.

2.	S = Goods V = must have. Revised: The transaction must be in writing for the sale of goods over five hundred dollars ($500.00).

3.	S = possibility V = is. Revised: The legislature revised the statute because it recognized the possibility that an intoxicated driver may decide to continue driving rather than be arrested after pulling over to the shoulder of the road.

4.	S = theory V = is. Revised: The "moral right doctrine" is another theory available to Mr. Henderson but not to his co-defendants.

5.	From Lloyd's statement to his tax preparer that "the lunches were really social," we can infer that Lloyd intentionally misrepresented at least some of the information.
OR Lloyd told his tax preparer that "the lunches were really social." That statement indicates that Lloyd intentionally misrepresented at least some of the information. (Some readers may not object to the original sentence because the quoted material helps to set off some of the intervening words.)

6.	S = reading V = favored. Revised: Despite its insistence that there was no accompanying oral agreement, the court read the written contract in a light most favorable to the tire manufacturer.

7. S = court V = stated. Revised: In another case involving the revision of a law manual, the court stated that "the purchase of a copyright did not carry with it a license to defame . . . ."

8. S = name and reputation V = have been injured. Revised: The libelous conduct of <u>Trade Union World</u> has injured our client's name and reputation as an upstanding citizen and honest businessman who treats his employees fairly.

9. S = concept V = suggests. Revised: When applied to the instant case, the concept of voluntary assumption of duty suggests that the State voluntarily assumed a duty to use due care in conducting inspections of nursing homes. (Also consider omitting "the concept of.")

10. S = argument V = is. Revised: The State may argue that it owes a duty only to the public generally and not to any individual, but such an argument is not persuasive. (Some readers may not object to the original sentence with the subject and verb far apart.)

✦EXERCISE 23.G   SUBJECT-VERB REVIEW

1. S-V distance; weak verb: action is buried in the noun "research."

   Revised: I have researched your potential claim . . .

   OR I have fully researched your potential claim . . . .

   OR I have completed my research on your claim . . . .

2.   weak subject: too abstract; weak verb: form of "to be."

Revised: My opinion is based on the current statutory provisions . . . . (This revision is

an effective use of passive voice.)

OR I base my opinion on the current statutory provisions.

3.   ineffective passive.

Revised: You terminated that lease . . . .

4.   ineffective passive. Note the compound verb

Revised: He received this notice of termination with at least 30 days' notice and accepted

it as valid.

5.   weak verbs: form of "to be." Note the compound verb.

Revised: As of September 10, 1985, you have not been reimbursed your $200.00 security

deposit, nor have you received any written explanation from your former landlord telling

why he has not returned the money. (This revision is an effective use of passive voice.)

OR As of September 10, 1985, your landlord has neither reimbursed your $200.00

security deposit nor has he sent you a written explanation of why he has not returned the

money.

6.   ineffective passive; S-V distance.

Revised: . . . you have sent four letters to Mr. Printer inquiring about your deposit.

7.   ineffective passive.

Revised: You left the apartment clean and undamaged.

8.   weak verb; S-V distance.

Revised: Under the relevant Iowa statute, you have a strong chance of recovering your deposit.

9.   weak verb: form of "to be"; action buried in noun "requirement."

Revised: Generally, the law requires that landlords. . . .

10.   passive.

Revised: Since Mr. Printer sent no refund or statement . . . .

✦EXERCISE 23.H SENTENCE LENGTH

1.   Traditionally, Florida courts have deferred to the legislature's policy judgment on the propriety of punitive damages award. They have manifested this deference by adhering rigidly to the rule that punitive damages should be awarded with the greatest caution and only where specifically authorized by statute.

2. In determining whether a private citizen is an instrument or agent of the government, the court will examine two critical factors: (1) the government's knowledge or acquiescence and (2) the intent of the party performing the search.

3. Infringement is an interference with the rights granted to another under a law, a regulation, or a contract. It is usually categorized as infringement of copyright, infringement of patents, or infringement of trademarks.
OR Infringement comprises three categories: infringement of copyrights, of patents, and of trademarks.

4. In *Board of Regents*, the court held that the trial court correctly withheld a jury instruction regarding arson from the jury. The court reasoned that the theory of arson was only a mere possibility and did not rise above speculation and conjecture.

5. In *E. I. duPont de Nemorus & Co., Inc. v. Christopher,* the defendants used an airplane to photograph the plaintiff's Beaumont, Texas plant. The plant contained, in an open area, a secret but thus far unpatented process for producing methanol. The process had been developed by duPont at considerable time and expense, and it had provided duPont with a significant advantage over its competitors.

6. The insurance adjustor testified that the defendant's brakes were not functioning properly. He based his conclusion upon a physical inspection of the accident area for skid marks

both the night of the accident and the next day during daylight. He found one distinct skid mark and one virtually non-existent skid mark.

7. Under a negligence per se or common law theory of negligence, is a tavern owner liable when he served alcohol to a minor without checking her identification, when he continued to serve her alcohol after she spilled a drink and sang while on top of a table, and when the car she was driving later collided with another vehicle, causing personal injury.

8. The plaintiff may obtain a summary of facts known and opinions held by the nontestifying expert by other means: through depositions of occupants of the cars or through another expert evaluating the facts and making a conclusion.

9. Under N.Y. Penal Law §125.25(3) (McKinney 1975), the felony murder rule, would a charge of second degree murder be valid when the defendant was one of three participants in a robbery, when the store owner had a previous heart condition, when the store owner subsequently died of a massive heart attack, and when his physician states that the stress of the robbery undoubtedly caused the heart attack.

10. Regardless of the victim's previous heart condition and the foreseeability of his death, the felony-murder rule applies for two reasons: 1) robbery is inherently dangerous and 2) a nexus has been established between the robbery and homicide.

Sentence one of paragraph one can be trimmed from 58 words to 31 words by eliminating unnecessary wordiness. Some writers may prefer to retain the date in the introductory phrase; others prefer to omit it because it is included in the citation.

Revised:

The Equal Credit Opportunity Act (ECOA) was enacted to ensure that all firms that

extend credit make that credit equally available to creditworthy customers without regard to sex

or marital status. (31 words)

Sentence two of paragraph one is somewhat long at 37 words. Although the commas separating the items in the series help to break up the sentence a bit, a colon provides a strong break between the first half of the sentence and the possible reasons for credit discrimination. Again, the date is included in the citation.

Revised:

The ECOA was later expanded to prohibit credit discrimination for the following reasons:

(13 words) race, color, national origin, age, receipt of public assistance income, or the exercise in

good faith of the rights guaranteed under the Consumer Credit Protection Act. (26 words).

Sentence three of paragraph two, originally a 40 word sentence, can be broken up into three shorter sentences.

Revised:

The ECOA was enacted as both a consumer protection statute and an antidiscrimination

statute. (14 words) As a consumer protection statute, the ECOA was designed to provide

accurate information to and about consumers involved in credit transactions. (21 words) As an antidiscrimination statute, the ECOA was designed to shield protected classes of consumers from credit discrimination. (17 words)

✦EXERCISE 23.J   SENTENCES REVIEW

1.   None of the sentences are overly long (22-10-33-16 words, respectively), and there seems to be sufficient variety in the sentence length. The one short sentence, however, emphasizes a point unfavorable to the client.

Revised:

Mr. Barker is a stable, loving father, who will provide a stimulating home environment for the Barkers' two children, George and Karen. Although the psychiatrist's report suggests that Mr. Barker may be compulsive, this trait is not unusual for highly successful businessmen. In fact, Mr. Barker's success in business gives him more flexibility in his work schedule. Consequently, he will have even more time for his children. Furthermore, the psychologist's report agrees that Mr. Barker has potential to be a sensitive, outgoing parent.

2.   None of the sentences are overly long (9-13-15-17 words, respectively), but they lack sufficient variety in sentence length to be interesting.

Revised:

Mrs. Barker's psychological stability, however, is far from certain. She has been diagnosed as having histrionic tendencies and as being mildly hysterical, two disorders which, according to her psychologist, make her prone to alcohol and chemical dependency. Once, this dependency became so severe that Mrs. Barker required medical care to cope with her alcoholism.

248

3.   The three sentences have variety in sentence length (35, 8, and 23 words respectively), and the second short sentence emphasizes a key point for the client. The first sentence, however, is unnecessarily long.

Revised:

Mrs. Barker may contend that the court should apply the tender years doctrine, which presumes that young children of "tender years" should be raised by the mother. The Barker children are not of tender years.

✦EXERCISE 23.K   SENTENCES REVIEW

Lester and Marie Franklin, plaintiffs, (Franklins) operate a combination grocery store and delicatessen at 704 Filbert Street, San Francisco, California. The store occupies premises owned by Tyler and Tina Morgan (Morgans).

On September 22, 1985, the Franklins and the Morgans entered into a lease agreement for the premises. The term of the lease was eighteen (18) years with an option to terminate at the end of ten (10) years. (See lease agreement attached as Exhibit A.) In essence, the lease provides for payment of base rent, percentage rent, taxes, and insurance. It also permitted the Franklins to perform tenant improvements as approved by the Morgans.

Additionally, under the lease (Ex. A Para. 5) the Franklins agreed to maintain and repair the premises but with some exceptions. The exceptions were the roof, exterior walls, and foundation. Maintenance and repair of these items were reserved to the Morgans and made their responsibility.

While the Franklins were making the pre-approved tenant improvements, the City of San Francisco performed an inspection and determined that the brick parapets needed seismic bracing. The brick parapets are part of the exterior wall above the roof line. Without this bracing, the City would not grant the final permit to allow the Franklins to open their business.

The seismic bracing was not part of the tenant improvements prepared by the Franklins and approved by the Morgans. Further, the seismic bracing was not required because of the character of the Franklins' business. It would have been required for any tenant.

At the time the City required the seismic bracing, the Morgans were unavailable, vacationing in Mexico. Consequently, they were not available to perform the repairs, although the lease provisions specifically reserved to the Morgans the responsibility for the exterior walls. The Franklins were now faced with being unable to open their business, thereby incurring substantial damages and possibly increased costs to perform the repairs. Instead the Franklins chose to pay for the repairs and then recoup the cost from the Morgans, pursuant to the lease terms.

The Franklins immediately paid the construction and engineering costs and sought reimbursement from the Morgans. The Morgans refused payment, contending that the Franklins accepted the premises "as is." The Morgans further contended that, although the bracing was required on a part of the structure specifically reserved to the Morgans, the bracing was not a repair.

At the time of the arbitration, the Franklins are seeking recovery from the Morgans for the amount to repair the exterior wall; the Morgans are seeking a judgment declaring that they are not responsible for the repair costs.

✦EXERCISE 23.L EMPHASIS

1.   When the police officers found her, the girl was wearing only her shoes and she was tied to a tree.

2.   When the police officers found her, the girl was tied to a tree and wearing only one item of clothing: her shoes.

3.   Seven people were killed on July 14, 1986, in a nuclear accident at Beatty, Nevada -- the first fatal accident at the Nevada site.

OR

The first fatal nuclear accident at the Beatty, Nevada site occurred on July 14, 1986, killing seven people.

4.   If the defendant is convicted of this offense, a judge has the option of imposing a fine not to exceed $5,000 and sentencing him to period of two to ten years.

5. The plaintiff's final argument will depend on whether he can prove a substantial depreciation -- over $20,000 -- of the value of his property.

OR

The plaintiff's final argument will depend on whether he can prove a depreciation of his property value of over $20,000.

6. Under the Uniform Building Code, the tenant has no maintenance obligations; the obligation to maintain the building falls on the owner.

7. Under the Uniform Building Code, the obligation to maintain the building falls on the owner, not the tenant.

8. We can prove that the dog is vicious: he has bitten three people.

9. The church freely admits that it operated a full time school without a special use permit.

10. The church operated a fulltime school without a special use permit--a point the church admits freely.

1. Although five witnesses have placed Sharon Clark at the scene of the crime, she still claims she was at home alone.

2. An explosives expert testified that any slight change in the cabin pressure would activate the detonator.

3. According to company regulations, no employee could leave his or her post until the supervisor on duty had assigned a replacement.

4. In the union's history, an allegation of this severity has never been made.

    OR

    Never before in the union's history has an allegation of this severity been made.

5. It was the deceased, not the defendant, who ran the stoplight.

6. All the bonds in the safety deposit box were under her name.

7. The bonds in the safety deposit box were under only her name.

    OR Only the bonds in the safety deposit box were under her name.

8.   Every member of the union voted to ratify the contract.

9.   Despite numerous warnings from the Environmental Protection Agency, National

Chemical still disposed of waste by-products by dumping them in the bay.

10.   Laura Smith died, not from the operation, but from inadequate post operative care.

✦EXERCISE 23.N CHANGING WORD ORDER

1.   In a lineup with no other bearded men, the defendant was later identified.

2.   The defendant--at gunpoint--forced Ms. Harper to perform fellatio.

3.   The starter's pistol has been identified by two witnesses as the weapon used.

4.   Only for a manifest abuse will the trial court's exercise of this discretion be overturned on

appeal.

5.   The burden of proof mere assertions do not satisfy.

6.   The defendant could have effectively corrected, at the time they were made, all alleged

errors.

7.   On each separate count, the State had strong evidence.

8.   The words "pistol" and "revolver" are included in the definition of deadly weapon.

9.   Also denied was the defendant's motion to sever Counts I and II from Counts III, IV, and V.

10.   On all five counts, the defendant was convicted by the jury.

✦EXERCISE 23.O   BREAKING A PATTERN

1.   Mr. Baylor's behavior shows a clear pattern: first, intimidating his children; then, intimidating his wife; and now, intimidating a witness.

2.   Thomas Dever was not insane when he threatened Miss Dever in October. He was not insane when he shadowed her for two weeks in November. And he was not insane when he brutally killed her on Christmas Eve.

3.   We want to believe that our country acted fairly. We want to believe that our country acted wisely. We do not want to believe that our country acted maliciously.

4.   After twenty years in prison, Carl Wilson returned to society without a job, without a

home, without a cent in the bank.

OR

. . . with no job, with no home, and with no money in the bank.

5.   All the opposition lacks is proof: proof that the defendant was at the scene of the crime,

proof that the defendant had a motive, and proof that the defendant committed the deed.

6.   No court, no jury, and no jail term will undo what Frank Morris has done.

7.   Desmond Adams rebuilt his business with his own money, with his own hard work, and

without the help of his former partner.

8.   It was Judith Davis, not Martin Davis, who refused to see a marriage counselor. It was

Judith Davis, not Martin Davis, who filed for a divorce. And now it is Judith Davis, not

Martin Davis, who wants an even larger share of her husband's pension.

9.   In the contract for the Lowell building, Kyle Davis had a silent partner: Ronald Thomas.

In the contract for the Madison complex, Kyle Davis had a silent partner: Ronald

Thomas. But in the contract for the Westside shopping mall, Kyle Davis acted alone.

10. With malice aforethought, Michael Mann bought the .38 caliber pistol at Seaside Pawn Shop. With malice aforethought, he waited in the car for Howard Peterson to return home from work. And with malice aforethought, Michael Mann followed Howard Peterson up to his first door and shot him three times in the chest.

✦**EXERCISE 24.A WORD CHOICE**

1. ~~exhibit~~ indicate, suggest, show, prove, establish
   ~~for~~ of

2. ~~constitute this as~~ determine, hold

3. ~~display~~ show

4. ~~have ... give to~~ order ... for ~~kids~~ children

5. ~~explored to find~~ looked to see ~~to~~ of

6. ~~tough~~ difficult ~~award~~ grant

7. ~~annunciated~~ enunciated

8. ~~ceased~~ was dissolved

9. ~~decreed~~ found (or simply awarded damages) ~~decreed~~
   granted

10. ~~set~~ created, established

11. ~~beyond~~ by

12. ~~dissent~~ descent

13. ~~exasperated~~ exacerbated

14. ~~evokes~~ invokes

15. ~~prodigy~~ progeny

A court will need to examine the tests for two doctrines, *respondeat superior* and "loaned servant," to determine whether Dr. Robinson or Bondurant Temporary Agency, Inc. (Bondurant) can be held vicariously liable for the complete destruction of Ms. Bakerman's coat. The first doctrine, *respondeat superior*, has a three-prong test. The first two prongs of the test are met. First, Carol Kester was negligent for the destruction of the coat. *See Nyman v. MacRae Bros. Constr. Co.*, 69 Wash. 2d 285, 287, 418 P.2d 253, 254 (1966). Second, Carol was acting within the scope of her employment at the time of the tortious act. *See Kuehn v. White*, 24 Wash. App. 274, 277, 600 P.2d 679, 682 (1979). There will be a dispute about the third **prong**: whether Carol was under the control of Bondurant, her general employer, or under the control of Dr. Robinson, her temporary employer at the time the coat was destroyed. *See Kroshus v. Koury*, 20 Wash. App. 258, 263, 633 P.2d 909, 911 (1981) (quoting *McLean v. St. Regis Paper Co.*, 6 Wash. App. 727, 732, 496 P.2d 571, 574 (1972)).

The second **doctrine**, "loaned servant," has a three-part test to determine who has control of a temporary employee. *Pichler v. Pacific Mechanical Constr.*, 1 Wash App. 447, 450-451, 462 P.2d 960, 963 (1969). The first and second parts of the test--who has the right to select or hire and fire the servant and who has the right to direct how the servant shall perform his duties--will be disputed, but the most important **part** will be who had exclusive control or the right to exclusive control at the time of the tortious act. *Pichler*, 1 Wash. App. at 450-451, 462 P.2d at 963.

1.   The grief over the loss of a six-week-old fetus is hardly comparable to the grief over the

loss of a viable fetus.

2.   This policy of protecting the **investor** from the various schemes devised by

promoters has been a persuasive cornerstone for judicial interpretation of **investment** contracts

in the post-*Howey* era. *See, e.g., SEC v. Glenn W. Turner Ent., Inc.*, 474 F.2d 476 9th Cir.

(1973). However, the Ninth Circuit apparently does not find **investor** protection alone

determinative when interpreting federal securities law. Other factors may come into play, such

as the underlying nature of the financial relationship between the **investor** and the promoter.

See, e.g. Brodt v. Bache & Co., Inc., 595 F.2d 459 9th Cir. (1978). Consequently, legal analysis

of CP's **investment** scheme does not yield a precise conclusion about whether a Ninth Circuit

federal court would deem it to be an **investment** contract.

3.   Correct. A case is compared with a case.

4.   A potential plaintiff would argue that the fetus is the personal property of the

mother. This argument would be similar to the **argument in** *Moore* in that the body part that

was surgically removed was the personal property of the plaintiff patient.

5.   In its decision, the *Brodt* court explicitly rejected using the concept of "horizontal

commonality" employed in other circuits; that **concept** would require that there be

a pooling of interests combined with a pro-rata sharing of profits. *Id.* at 460. Instead, the court

used the broader **concept** of "vertical commonality," which requires that the investor and the

promoter be involved in some common venture without mandating that other investors also be

involved in the venture. *Id.* at 461

(citing *Hector v. Wiens*, 533 F.2d 429 (9th Cir. 1976).

Note: Although most readers would not have a problem with the synonym "approach," it is more precise to retain the earlier term "concept." "Concept" must replace "principle" so that "horizontal commonality" and "vertical commonality" are properly compared.

◆EXERCISE 24.D SUBJECT-VERB-OBJECT COMPARISONS

1. language has broadened
   [subject] [verb]

   Revision: Since then, the courts' interpretation of the language has broadened.

2. *Eggert* says
   [subject] [verb]

   Revision: As for the burden of proof, the *Eggert* court says that the burden is on the plaintiff to establish a right to maintain the action in an action for conversion.

3. weight (of case law) would deny relief
   [subject] [verb] [object]

   Revision: Should Mr. Robinson bring suit, a court is likely to deny him relief based upon the great weight of the case law.

4. conviction has been interpreted
   [subject] [verb]

   Revision: Courts in the fourth circuit have interpreted § 1071 as requiring proof of four elements for a conviction: 1) that a federal warrant had been issued for the fugitive's arrest; 2) that the defendant had knowledge that a warrant had been issued for the fugitive's arrest; 3) that the defendant actually harbored or concealed the fugitive; and 4) that defendant intended to prevent the fugitive's discovery or arrest.

5.   (issues) that   argue
        [subject]   [verb]

   Revision: There are persuasive arguments based on public policy for restricting a woman's right to fetal tissue.

6.   test   is determined (by the use)
        [subject] [verb]

   Revision: To determine whether a nuisance exists, the court considers the use to which the property is put.

7.   likelihood   is (favorable)
        [subject]   [verb]

   Revision: The court is likely to determine that this is an established custodial environment.

8.   doctrine withheld property
        [subject] [verb]   [object]

   Revision: Under the trust fund doctrine, which was created by the equity courts to protect creditors when an indebted corporation dissolved, the corporation's property was withheld to pay off debts.

9.   New Age aerobics may (not) be causing hazards congestion buildings
        [subject]   [verb]   [objects]

     Note that the subject and verb must match each of the objects. Can New Age aerobics cause a building?

   Revision: Even though New Age aerobics may not be responsible for safety hazards, increased traffic congestion, or unsightly buildings, the cumulative effects of its activities should be considered.

10.   probability   is (unlikely)
         [subject]   [verb]

Revision: Mrs. Davis probably cannot meet this required standard of proof.

✦EXERCISE 24.E   GRAMMATICAL AMBIGUITIES

See Answer Key for exercises 26.L, 26.M, 26.N, and 26.O.

✦EXERCISE 24.F   CONCISENESS

1.   Two defenses are available to Acme. OR Acme has two available defenses.

2.   You are probably bound by the written agreement simply because you signed it.

3.   In determining whether there was a sudden emergency, courts also consider

whether there was sufficient warning that should have alerted the driver to the imminent

danger. (It is effective to keep both *there was* expletives because the point of the sentence

is the existence of a sudden emergency and the existence of sufficient warning.)

4.   The court will liberally construe Fed. R. Civ. P. 4(d)(1).

5.   The court may follow the view that "in a highly mobile and affluent society, it is

unrealistic to interpret 4(d)(1) so that the person to be served has only one dwelling house

or usual place of abode at which process may be left." 4A Charles Alan Wright & Arthur

R. Miller, Federal Practice and Procedures §1096, (2d ed.)

6.   The two parties differ over whether the deposit is refundable.

7.   The court inferred that because the papers were left with appellant's mother, the

appellant received them.

8.   If "substantial" is held to be analogous with "principal," then five per cent of a total

business would be the minimum necessary to establish that certain sales of merchandise are a "principal" part of a business.

9.   We could argue that Ms. Fox so conditioned her acceptance of your offer as to create a
      counteroffer.

10.   The legislature intended to encourage corporations to explore new ways of reducing
      energy costs.

11.   After thoroughly researching your complaint against Mr. Brown, I conclude that the best
      way to recover the $2500 that he owes you is to file a lien against his orchard.

12.   The boys deny making any threats.

13.   The defendant has moved to suppress the evidence seized after the arrest.

14.   The trial court did not err in failing to instruct on the absence of intervening cause.

✦EXERCISE 24.G   CONCISENESS

1.   Before I can advise you, I need to ask whether your husband knew that his life
      expectancy was short.

2.   In addition to the procedure that begins the process, the plant foreman must then start
      the back-up system.

3.   The night watchman usually ends his rounds at 5 a.m. after inspecting each safe in the
      building.

4.   Before trial, the defendant will file a Motion in Limine to exclude evidence of his prior
      convictions.

5.   The consensus among the board members was that having employees follow a certain

procedure when they entered or left the building would not end employee theft.

6. The Parkers assumed that real estate agents who list a home for sale are obligated to appraise that home.

7. For two months during 1985, Mr. Wilson aided a known felon by allowing her to use his cabin to hide from the police.

8. There is no constitutional right to receive credit, but much can be done to insure that credit availability is fair.

9. In my opinion, we cannot get an injunction to eliminate the factory's noon whistle.

10. We ordered the building vacated so that the inhabitants would be safe.

✦EXERCISE 24.H - CONCISENESS

1. In late October 1987, Kyle Nelson asked Frances Miles, an acquaintance, to house sit for him while he was away on vacation.

2. The trial judge calculated O'Hara's offender score as seven, basing her decision on Or. Rev. Stat. §137.370 (4), which states in part that "[u]nless the court expressly orders otherwise, a term of imprisonment shall be concurrent with the remainder of any sentence previously imposed at the time the court imposes sentence."

3. Instruction 10 did not shift the ultimate burden of proof to Chin, create any mandatory presumption, or impose any burden of producing evidence on Chin. Rather, the instruction states that the presumption "is not binding" upon the jury and that the jury can determine "what weight, if any," to give to the presumption.

266

4. At the disposition hearing, the state presented a document describing Ortega's prior criminal history: ten burglary convictions and three minor offenses subject to diversion.

5. Peters moved to Chesterville to be near her husband, who was an inmate at the state penitentiary at Chesterville. Upon arriving in Chesterville, Peters met a woman whose husband was also an inmate in the penitentiary.

6. The legislature directed the Department of Ecology to publish a statutorily prescribed notice by four different means: 1) publication of the notice once a year for five years in major as well as local newspapers; 2) publication of the notice every six months on radio and television stations broadcasting in every county; and 3) posting the notice in a conspicuous location in every county; and 4) including a copy of the notice with notices of taxes due for 1972 mailed by each county treasurer.

7. The Court of Appeals upheld the rape conviction and corresponding habitual criminal finding but reversed the assault conviction.

8. At 2:20 a.m. on September 29, 1986, Brian Smith entered his parents' bedroom where they were sleeping. Brian shot his mother in the head with a 30.06 rifle, killing her. Mr. Smith woke up and saw Brian leave the bedroom. Unable to telephone for help because Brian had taken the telephone off the hook in the kitchen, Mr. Smith locked the bedroom door and escaped through the window. Brian returned to the bedroom, intending to kill his father, but found that he had escaped.

9. Upon arriving at the scene, the officers discovered Barbara Wilson-Hughes in a comatose condition and immediately called an emergency medical unit. The medical unit transported Mrs. Wilson-Hughes to a local hospital where she was treated for a "closed-

head injury" and several facial lacerations.

10.   In *Workman*, the court set forth a two-prong test for determining when lesser offense

instructions should be given: 1) each element of the lesser offense must be a necessary

element of the offense charged; 2) evidence must support an inference that the lesser

crime was committed.

✦EXERCISE 24.I CONCISENESS REVIEW

1.   Each plaintiff received $20,000 in damages.

2.   A driver who refuses to wear prescription glasses and who drives faster than the speed

limit is a hazard.

3.   Trooper Evans, who investigated the accident, testified that the "primary casual factor" of

the accident had been the defendant's intoxicated state.

4.   Jones will argue that he did not knowingly and voluntarily consent to Officer Smith's

search of his wallet. Jones will further argue that the items discovered during the search,

particularly the stolen charge card, exceeded the scope of his consent.

5.   Henson responded to the public disclosure request by providing all documents, except

two letters, which were excluded because they contained proprietary or private

information about Henson's business practices.

6.   Mail was sent to their separate addresses, but on occasion an invitation addressed to both

of them would come to Mr. Jones's address.

7. Mr. McRae stated that he discussed only the manufacture and delivery of the equipment with Jim Drane, the principal of Lakeland Elementary, and reiterated that they did not discuss installation.

8. Recognizing that in similar cases courts have issued directed verdicts, I expect that you will also get a directed verdict.

9. The court correctly denied the defendant's motion for a new trial because the defendant must suggest more than a "possibility of prejudice."

10. Because my client was uninformed about the law and because she is elderly, this court should grant her special consideration. She wants only to give her prized hand-painted china collection to her community library.

✦EXERCISE 24.J CONCISENESS REVIEW

1. "[C]omfortable enjoyment means both mental quiet and physical comfort." *Park v. Stolzheise*, 24 Wash. 2d 781, 167 P.2d 412 (1946). The neighbors will argue that floodlights on until midnight adversely affects their physical comfort because their sleep is disturbed by the lights beaming through the bedroom windows. To support this contention, the neighbors will use *Bruskland* where the court stated that automobile headlights shining upon a bedroom window constituted a private nuisance because they unreasonably interfered with owners' comfortable enjoyment of the property. 42 Wash. 2d at 348. Consequently, the trier of fact will probably rule that the floodlights interfered with the neighbors' comfortable enjoyment of their property.

2. In addition, the court must determine whether the plaintiff "thrust into the controversy in an attempt to influence the outcome." *Hutchinson*, 443 U.S. at 135. For example, the *Waldbaum* court held that the plaintiff had thrust into a controversy in an attempt to influence its outcome when the plaintiff invited both the press and the public to a special meeting it held to discuss the introduction of unit pricing and open dating into supermarkets.

3.   Although the two levels of immunity have been well defined, the level of immunity that parole board members should be afforded remains unclear. To analyze the case at hand, the court must examine those decisions of the Supreme Court, Third Circuit, and Ninth Circuit concerning the levels of immunity accorded to public officials that present the tests to determine the type and scope of immunity that the Board members should be afforded.

✦EXERCISE 24.K   LEGALESE

Dear Mr. Patterson:

Enclosed is a copy of the Notice of Appeal that was filed with the King County Superior Court on November 25. This notice will be immediately sent to the Court of Appeals.

Because your case involves your constitutional rights, the Court of Appeals will do a *de novo* review of your case; that is, the Court will do a "fresh" review of the entire case as though there had been no trial court decision. Unfortunately, however, we are unlikely to win at appellate court level. As we have discussed before, show-ups are not automatically impermissible. As a result, the Court of Appeals will need, among other things, to balance the suggestiveness of the show-up with the reliability of the identifications. In other words, the appellate court will

This exercise should be done after reading Section 24.1.7 in the *Handbook*.

Review exercises 26.L, 26.M, 26.N, and 26.O of the *Practice Book* on dangling and misplaced modifiers.

✦EXERCISE 24.L GENDER-NEUTRAL LANGUAGE

1.   masked intruder OR masked robber OR masked and armed assailant. (If the person is masked, the sex is probably unknown.)

2.   neighbor. (If the wife lives with her husband, she is a neighbor as well.)

3.   the human family

4.   Dear Members of the Board OR Dear Board Members

5.   the driver in the second vehicle.

1.   The operator of the vehicle left the scene without identifying herself or himself.

2.   When determining the status of a child as Indian, the state court must seek verification of the child's status from either the Bureau of Indian Affairs or from the child's tribe.

3.   Evidence of other offenses may not be admitted as proof of the charged offense if the evidence is relevant only to show the defendant's criminal disposition.

4.   A guardian is a person lawfully invested with the power, and charged with the duty, of taking care of another who, for defect of age, understanding, or self-control, is considered unable to administer his or her own affairs.

5.   Summary judgment should be denied if the moving party does not sustain its initial burden of proof and if reasonable persons would reach different conclusions from the evidence presented.

6.   When requesting that a judgment be set aside, the moving party's attorney must comply with CR 60(e)(1), which requires an affidavit setting forth the facts constituting a defense.

7.   The statute gives husbands and wives more freedom to independently dispose of their property by contract, free from court supervision. OR The statute gives marital partners....

8.   Mrs. Edwards is a mother who works outside of the home and who has little time or energy left for her children at the end of the day. Mr. Edwards, on the other hand, operates his accounting business out of his home. Consequently, he is able to give the children the care they need.

9.   The Acme Loan Service informed Mr. and Mrs. Valdez that the liens would have to be removed before they could secure a loan.

10.   "It is the purpose of this subchapter to assure a meaningful disclosure of credit terms so that the consumer[s] will be able to compare more readily the various credit terms available to . . . [them] and avoid the uninformed use of credit, and to protect the consumer[s] against inaccurate and unfair credit billing and credit card practices." 15 U.S.C. §1601 (a).

11.   Rule 9 of the Admission to Practice Rules provides that qualified law students, law clerks, or law school graduates may be granted a limited license to practice law if they 1) have completed at least two-thirds of a three-year course of studies, 2) have the written

approval of their law school dean, and 3) have certified that they have read and are familiar with the Rules of Professional Conduct.

12.   Helene Russell was a pharmacist in Baton Rouge, Louisiana, when a federal grand jury indicted her on fifteen counts of violating Title 21 U.S.C. §§ 841(a)(1), 841(b)(2), 843(a)(4), and 827(a)(3).

13.   The comment to subsection (a) of §158 explains that a person may invade another's property by "throwing, propelling, or placing a thing" either on the land or in the air above it.

14.   The airline's representative claimed that no one could have prevented the tragedy and that the accident was "an act of God."

15.   The court may impose an exceptional sentence for the offense of indecent liberties when the victim is particularly vulnerable or unable to resist because of young age and when the offender is not amenable to treatment.

✦EXERCISE 24.N GENDER-NEUTRAL LANGUAGE

1.   The incident giving rise to the attempted rape charge occurred on November 1, 1988, when the defendant, Harold Strickland went out on a date with Connie Osburn. About 12:30 a.m., Strickland drove Osburn back to his apartment. Once inside, Strickland immediately forced Osburn into the bedroom and onto the bed. Without her consent, he lay on top of her and tried to force his hand under her clothing.

Osburn then convinced Strickland that she needed to use the bathroom. He relented and, while she was in the bathroom, Osburn escaped through a window. After finding a police officer, Osburn took her to the scene and showed her Strickland's apartment.

✦EXERCISE 26.A FRAGMENTS

1. <u>If the court allows the prior convictions to be admitted into evidence</u> is a fragment because "if" makes the clause dependent. It should be attached to the preceding sentence.

    <u>Possible revision</u>: The defendant's story will not be told if the court allows the prior convictions to be admitted into evidence.

2. <u>Which generally gives a person worldwide recognition for his or her work</u> is a fragment because "which" makes it a dependent clause. It should be attached to the preceding sentence.

    <u>Possible revision</u>: Mr. Barnett won a Pulitzer prize, which generally gives a person worldwide recognition for his or her work.

3. Both sentences are complete sentences.

4. <u>The second interest, honor and reputation</u> is a fragment because it lacks a verb.
    <u>Possible revision</u>: The second interest <u>is</u> honor and reputation.

5. <u>Therefore, probably not of probative value to the state's case</u> is a fragment because it lacks both a subject and a verb.

    <u>Possible revision</u>: Therefore, <u>they are</u> probably not of probative value to the state's case.

6. <u>Especially in the light of potential service in New York under the California long arm statute</u> is a fragment because it lacks both a subject and a verb. It should be attached to the preceding sentence.

    <u>Possible revision</u>: Although a technical case can be made for non-compliance with Rule 4(d)(1), the question of the overall efficiency of this approach is open to doubt, especially in the light of potential service in New York under the California long arm statute.

7. <u>The trend in American courts to balance economic and moral interests in the areas of contract and tort law</u> is a fragment. It lacks a verb.

Possible revision: The trend in American courts is to balance economic and moral interests in the areas of contract and tort law.

8. Whether the Los Angeles home is the dwelling house of the defendant is a fragment because "whether" makes the clause dependent. The exception for issue statements does not apply here because this sentence would appear in the text and not be set apart as a formal issue statement.

    Possible revision: The court has only one real issue to decide: whether the Los Angeles home is the dwelling house of the defendant.

9. Unfair competition, a general term, embracing the narrower area of trademark law, which concerns the same legal wrong, namely, misrepresentations as to the source of goods or services is a fragment because it lacks a verb. Embracing is a participle.

    Possible revision: Unfair competition is a general term, embracing the narrower area of trademark law, which concerns the same legal wrong, namely, misrepresentations as to the source of goods or services.

10. Whereas Ms. Patten alleges that she was robbed is a fragment because of the subordinating conjunction "whereas."

    Possible revision: The defendant states that Ms. Patten gave the coins to him as a gift, whereas Ms. Patten alleges that she was robbed.

◆EXERCISE 26.B FRAGMENTS

The following are fragments:

-   Which the Hoffelmeirs were emotionally attached to and considered a member of the family
-   Although Mrs. Kravitz tried to shoo the cat away
-   Within 36 hours after impoundment and despite a city ordinance that states that an impounded dog must be held for at least 72 hours before it can be destroyed

Possible Revision (changes are in boldface):

Agnes and Arthur Hoffelmeir were on vacation between October 11 and October 20, 1985. Their neighbors, the Burgesses, offered to take care of their pet cat, **which the Hoffelmeirs were emotionally attached to and considered a member of the family.**

On October 19, 1985, the cat went into Mrs. Kravitz's rose garden and began chewing the rose bushes. **Although Mrs. Kravitz tried to shoo the cat away, t**he cat kept returning to the Kravitz yard to chew on the rose bushes. Because this had happened on several other occasions, Mrs. Kravitz called the Humane Society.

The Humane Society impounded the cat, and Mr. Janske of the Society tried unsuccessfully to contact the Hoffelmeirs. The cat was destroyed on October 20, 1985, **within 36 hours after impoundment and despite a city ordinance that states that an impounded dog must be held for at least 72 hours before it can be destroyed.**

✦EXERCISE 26.C FRAGMENTS REVIEW

The following are fragments:

- If they both were bound by the Sequim City Ordinance

- And because the cat was destroyed before the time provided by the ordinance

- First, that *Sequin* refers to the unlawful garnishment or seizure of property, not the destruction of it

- Second, that they acted within their legal duty when the cat was seized

- Also because Mr. Janske attempted to contact the Hoffelmeirs before the cat was destroyed

- The Society and Mr. Janske being aware that pets are valuable to their owners

- The city ordinance's requirement for a holding period so that pet owners will have an opportunity to claim their pets

- Third, given that the rationale against awarding punitive damages is that an injured party will be adequately compensated through other measures

- And given that the replacement cost of the cat is not adequate compensation

Possible revision (changes are in boldface type):

In *Sequin*, a federal customs official impounded the plaintiff's car and failed to release her car in a timely manner. The court held that if the defendant's conduct could be interpreted as willful or malicious, the plaintiff could recover damages for emotional distress. *Id.* at 811.

We could argue that **if both the Humane Society and Mr. Janske were bound by the**

Sequim City Ordinance, they acted unlawfully because the cat was destroyed before the time provided by the ordinance.

The Humane Society and Mr. Janske may make the following arguments. First, *Sequin* **refers to the unlawful garnishment or seizure of property, not the destruction of it.** Second, **they acted within their legal duty when the cat was seized.** Third, because they did not intentionally violate the city ordinance **and because Mr. Janske attempted to contact the Hoffelmeirs before the cat was destroyed,** their actions were not willful or malicious.

The Hoffelmeirs could counter these claims with the following arguments. First, the seizure of the cat may have been lawful. The destruction was not. **(The preceding sentence is correct and not a fragment, even though the word "lawful" is elliptical.)** While *Sequin* is concerned with the unlawful seizure of property, the unlawful destruction of property is even more serious. Therefore, the principle of *Sequin* should apply in this case.

Second, the destruction of the cat before the proscribed time period is malicious and willful misconduct. The Society and Mr. Janske **are** aware that pets are valuable to their owners. Mr. Janske should have waited until the Hoffelmeirs were contacted before the cat was destroyed. **(or "Being aware that pets are valuable to their owners, Mr. Janske should have waited until the Hoffelmeirs were contacted before the cat was destroyed.")** The city ordinance **requires** a holding period so that pet owners will have an opportunity to claim their pets. If the Humane Society had abided by the ordinance, the cat would have been claimed, and the Hoffelmeirs would not have suffered this loss.

Third, given that the rationale against awarding punitive damages is that an injured party will be adequately compensated through other measures **and given that the replacement cost of the cat is not adequate compensation,** the only way the Hoffelmeirs will receive adequate compensation is through an award of damages that includes compensation for mental anguish.

Finally, there is persuasive authority to support the Hoffelmeirs' argument for damages for mental anguish. In a Louisiana case, a neighbor trapped the plaintiff's pet cat and brought it to the animal control center where the cat was destroyed. The plaintiffs sued to recover damages for the mental anguish and humiliation they suffered from the loss of their cat. The court held that if the plaintiffs suffered actual damages, they could be compensated for their mental anguish. *Peloquin v. Calcasier Parish Police Jury*, 367 So.2d 1246, 1251 (La. App. 1979).

✦EXERCISE 26.D   VERB TENSE

1.   The issue in *Farny* **was** whether the New Jersey address **was** the dwelling house or usual place of abode of the defendant. (Use simple past tense for the facts of an analogous case

when you do not have to differentiate between the time when the facts occurred and the time when the court proceedings occurred.)

2.   In *Farny,* the plaintiff **contended** that the New Jersey address **continued** to be defendant's dwelling house or usual place of abode. (Use simple past tense for the facts of an analogous case when you do not have to differentiate between the time when the facts occurred and the time when the court proceedings occurred.)

3.   Correct as is. Use simple present tense for general truths.

4.   Correct as is. Use simple past "held" and "was permissible" for court proceedings; use past perfect "had asked" for facts of analogous case.

5.   Just as the "present" may be a fraction of a second or several centuries long, the "simple past" may include the time period of both the facts and the court proceedings, or it may include just the court proceedings, depending on how the writer sets the sentence up. The sentence is correct as is, if the writer decided to make both the court proceedings and the facts of the analogous case in the simple past.

```
_____X_____X_____
        time period
          of court proceedings
          and facts of analogous case
```

If, however, the writer feels that it would help the reader to differentiate between the times of the court proceedings and the facts, simple past tense should be used for the court proceedings and past perfect tense should be used for the facts.

```
___X_____X_____X_____
  facts              court              the
  of analogous     proceedings        present
  case
```

Possible Revision:

In *Kraus*, the court held that the showup had not been impermissibly suggestive when the victim of an attempted robbery **had been** asked to identify the suspect after the police brought the suspect to the victim's place of business and when the police **had** conducted a pat-down search of the suspect in front of the victim.

6.   Correct as is. Use present tense to express a general truth.

7.   In *Bishop*, the court analyzed the predecessor to the current assault statute and concluded that aiming or discharging a firearm **is** not a lesser included offense of second degree assault. (Use present tense for a general truth.)

8.   Correct as is. Although the verb tense changes three times in this one sentence, from simple present to simple past to past perfect, the changes all correctly correspond to changes in time.

9.   Correct as is. "Held" and "must be read" are simple past tense; "had been written" is past perfect tense.

10.   Officer Thompson arrived at the scene of an accident in which a car towing a small trailer **had gone** over an embankment. (Past perfect needed for second verb.)

✦EXERCISE 26.E   VERB TENSE

In 1956, Bob Rhumb built the Cummings's house. In May 1957, Rhumb **built** a garage and fence, and John Miller **bought** the lot north of Rhumb's lot--the lot that is now Walker's--and **built** a house on it that was completed toward the end of 1957.

When Rhumb finished building his garage and fence, he **planted** his lawn, which extends* along a line from the fence to the street. Rhumb did not plant the three-foot strip that is now in dispute.

In the spring of 1958, Miller **planted** that strip with grass after Rhumb agreed to pay for a portion of the costs. In addition, along the back portion of his property, Miller **planted** a garden that extends* onto the three-foot strip.

From the time that Miller planted the lawn and garden in 1958 up to the present, he and the subsequent owners **have maintained** the garden and **mowed**** the grass on the strip that is now in dispute.

During the time that he had owned the property, Rhumb never **discussed** the true boundary line with anyone, except for references to it on two occasions: once, in 1958, when he agreed with Miller to pay a portion of the grass seed costs, and again in 1973, during Kaiser's ownership, when Kaiser was out washing his car, he said something to Rhumb like "Hey, you oughta come over and wash my car 'cause I always mow your lawn."

In January 1978, the Kaisers sold the property to the Hemstads. The Hemstads **lived** there until 1982 and then **rented** the house from 1982 until 1985, when they **sold** it to Debbie Walker. Walker and her predecessors have all maintained the garden and mowed the lawn just as the Millers did.

In 1989, our client, Charlie Cummings and his wife Anna **bought** the house previously occupied by Bob Rhumb. Cummings wants to remodel the house and replace the original garage, but the structure will be located about three feet north of the existing garage and fence. Debbie Walker has protested that the new structures, as described by our client, will be partially built on her property. Cummings has pointed out that the real property line **was located** three feet north of the existing garage and fence, but Debbie Walker is attempting to obtain title by claiming adverse possession.

* Use present tense "extends" if the lawn and garden are still to this day performing this action; use "extended" if the action was completed in the past.

** It is not necessary to write "have mowed." The "have" from "have maintained" carries over to the "mowed."

◆EXERCISE 26.F   SUBJECT-VERB AGREEMENT

1.	were	See Rule 4. *All* refers to the plural *justices.*
2.	were	See Rule 8. Delayed subject is *acts.*
3.	outlaws	See Rule 1. The intervening words introduced by *as well as* do not make the subject plural.
4.	are	See Rule 8. Normal word order is inverted for emphasis. *Parts* is the subject.
5.	has	See Rule 5. The members of the collective noun *majority* are acting as one unit.
6.	is	See Rule 4. *All* refers to the singular *evidence.*
7.	claims	See Rule 1. The intervening words do not make the subject plural.
8.	is	See Rule 7. The verb agrees with the subject *problem*, not the subject complement *employees.*
9.	was	See Rule 9. Words used as words are considered singular.
10.	considers	See Rules 1 and 5. The intervening words do not make the subject plural. Collective nouns acting as one unit, here *appellate court*, are singular.
11.	raise	See Rule 1. *Injuries* is a plural subject; the intervening words do not change its number.
12.	are	See Rules 2 and 7. The plural subject, *Reversing . . . and remanding . . .*, requires a plural verb. The verb agrees with the subject, not the subject complement, *only proper course of action.*
13.	is	See Rule 1. *Case* is the subject.
14.	was	See Exception B to Rule 2.

15.	has	See Rules 3 and 4. The verb must agree with the part of the subject after *nor*, which is *any*, a singular indefinite pronoun.
16.	are	See Rule 1. *Procedures* is the subject.
17.	has	See Rule 1, especially the Note. *Affidavit* is the subject.
18.	publishes	See Rules 9 and 10. *Which* refers back to the title of a magazine, which is always singular.
19.	refers	See Rule 9. *Prior unrelated matters* are words used as words.
20.	was	See Exception B of Rule 2.

◆EXERCISE 26.G PRONOUN AGREEMENT

1. See Rule 4. *Appellate court* is a collective noun acting as one unit; consequently, it requires the singular pronoun *it*, not *they*.

2. See Rule 1. *Witness* is singular, so it requires a singular pronoun. Possible corrections include replacing *their* with *his or her* or changing *a witness* to the plural form *witnesses*.

3. See Rule 3. *Someone* is an indefinite pronoun that requires a singular pronoun. *His* is singular, but it suggests that all obscene phone callers are male. Replace *his* with *his or her*.

4. See Rule 1. *Plaintiff* is singular, so it requires a singular pronoun. Possible corrections include replacing *their* with *his or her,* changing *plaintiff* to the plural form *plaintiffs*, or replacing *their* with *a*.

5. See Rule 1. *Tax consultant* is singular, so it requires a singular pronoun. The best correction is to change *tax consultant* to the plural form *tax consultants*. Changing the pronouns *they* and *them* to singular would require a rather awkward *he or she* and *him or her*.

6. Correct. See Rule 2. The pronoun *their* agrees with the nearer antecedent *companions*.

7. See Rule 4. *Board* is a collective noun acting as one unit; consequently, it requires the singular pronoun *its*, not *their*.

8. See Rule 3. *Somebody* is an indefinite pronoun that requires a singular pronoun. Replace *their* with *his or her*.

9. Correct. See Rule 1. *Parents and their daughter* is a plural subject requiring a plural pronoun.

10. See Rule 4. *IRS* is a collective noun acting as one unit; consequently, it requires the singular pronoun *it*, not *they*.

11. See Rule 1. The writer of this sentence managed to make the first set of pronouns *he or she* agree with the singular noun *party*, but then used the plural pronoun *their* later in the sentence. However, replacing *their* with *his or her* would make the sentence awkward. The best correction is to replace *party* with *parties* and *he or she* with *their*.

12. See Rule 4. *Harrison Tractor Company* is a collective noun acting as one unit; consequently, it requires the singular pronoun *it*, not *they*.

13. Correct. See Rule 1.

14. See Rule 4. *Jury* is a collective noun acting as one unit; consequently, it requires the singular pronoun *its*, not *their*.

15. See Rule 1. *Polygraph examination* is singular, so it requires a singular pronoun. The best correction is to replace *they* with either *polygraph examinations* or *such examinations*.

16. See Rule 3. *Everyone* is an indefinite pronoun that requires a singular pronoun. Replace *their* with *his or her*.

17. See Rules 2 and 4. The plural pronoun *they* does not agree with the nearer antecedent *friend*. To correct this sentence and make it more readable, begin by replacing *team* with *teammates*. Now, following the note in Rule 2, reorder the subject of the sentence so that it reads *neither his friend nor his teammates*. Now *they* correctly agrees with *teammates*. (The verb should also be changed to *are*.)

18. See Rule 4. *Court* is a collective noun acting as one unit; consequently, it requires the singular pronoun *it*, not *they*.

19. See Rule 1. Although the singular pronoun *his* agrees with the singular antecedent *perpetrator*, it suggests that the perpetrator leaving fingerprints on the window is male. Replace *his* with *his or her*.

20. See Rule 1. *Person* is singular, so it requires a singular pronoun. Possible corrections include replacing *their* with *his or her* or changing *person* to the plural form *persons*.

1. Howard Davis claims that the apartment manager yelled "Stop!" but never made an effort to interfere. OR Howard Davis claims that he never made an effort to interfere, although he heard the apartment manager yell "Stop!"

2. Davidson cooperated in the search by telling the police about the money and plane ticket under the false bottom of his suitcase. Davidson asserts that the ticket was from a recent trip to California. (If *it* is supposed to refer back to both the money and the plane ticket, then this sentence has an agreement problem [see section 7.4] and should be revised as follows: Davidson asserts that both were from a recent trip to California.)

3. Two brothers, Earl and Mason Hargrove, own two lumber yards, Eastside Building Supplies and Hargrove Lumber and Hardware. Both men are financially stable. OR Both lumberyards are financially stable.

4. O'Brien jammed the coins back behind the car seat and then hid the guns under the spare tire. After a brief search of the vehicle, the coins (or the guns) were found by Officer Martinez. OR O'Brien jammed the coins back behind the car seat and then hid the guns under the spare tire. After a brief search of the vehicle, both the coins and guns were found by Officer Martinez.

5. Juror Marc Stein stated to all other jurors that he had discussed the accident with his brother-in-law, a professional truck driver, who said that the accident could not have occurred as the defendant testified. OR Juror Marc Stein stated to all other jurors that he had discussed the accident with his brother-in-law, a professional truck driver. Stein added that the accident could not have occurred as the defendant testified.

6. After giving chase, Officer Conner apprehended Helman, who had a red bandanna scarf wrapped around a hand with some glass fragments in it. OR After giving chase, Officer Conner apprehended Helman. Wrapped around Helman's hand was a red bandanna scarf containing some glass fragments.

7. A claim by Stravinski that he was not present at the scene of the crime is not necessarily antagonistic with a claim by McDonald that Stravinski was present but did not commit the crime. OR Stravinski claims that he was not present at the scene of the crime, and McDonald admits to being present at the scene of the crime but denies committing the crime. These two claims are not necessarily antagonistic.

8. After conducting a pat-down search of the defendant, Deputy Peterson found a razor blade wrapped in a tissue under his own patrol car. OR After conducting a pat-down

search of the defendant, Deputy Peterson found a razor blade wrapped in a tissue under the defendant's vehicle.

9.   Edna Lino testified that several men, including James Crowell, approached the petitioner after he slapped her. She further testified that the petitioner appeared to be afraid that Crowell would beat him up. OR Edna Lino testified that several men, including James Crowell, approached the petitioner after he slapped her. She further testified that Crowell appeared to be afraid that the petitioner would beat him up.

10.   Clyde Reeves and his son, Daryl, were both injured in two automobile accidents that occurred within two months of each other. The first accident occurred on October 8, 1987, when Clyde was injured in a rear end collision with a vehicle driven by Melvin Maye. Clyde immediately sought and received medical care for the injuries from Dr. Charles Santino, his family physician. Later, on November 10, 1987, while still under Dr. Santino's care, he was involved in an accident with a vehicle driven by Carter Szabo. Clyde again sought and received medical treatment from Dr. Santino.

✦EXERCISE 26.1 BROAD PRONOUN REFERENCE

1.   In *Colorado Carpet*, the court held that an oral contract for ordinary carpet was unenforceable. The *Colorado Carpet* court reasoned that there was no evidence to indicate that the carpet was specially made for the buyer because it could be found in other retail outlets. The defendant tried to use this reasoning to say that the towels, like the carpet, are not special.

2.   The defense could bring up evidence of large sales of happy face items during the happy face fad several years ago. However, the happy face fad no longer exists, a fact that weakens this argument. OR This is a weak argument, however, because the happy face fad no longer exists.

3.   When the defense counsel addressed the subject of silence during direct examination of the defendant, she opened the door for a further development of the subject.

4.   The trial court admitted the defendant's prior convictions for theft because they proved only that the defendant acted in conformity with his propensity to commit crimes. ER 404(b) prohibits admitting evidence for such a reason.

5.   The destruction of the rosebushes could be classified as permanent. Such a classification would make the school district liable for the difference in the value of the Archers' property before and after the damage.

6. The Washington State Constitution expressly forbids the in-court questioning of witnesses about their religious beliefs for the purpose of affecting the weight of their testimony. Wash. Const. art. I, §11. This absolute prohibition is repeated and underscored by Washington Rule of Evidence 610.

7. In the instant case, the prosecution asked the prosecuting witness several questions about her religious activities, beliefs, and opinions, bolstering her credibility with the jury at the expense of Mr. Doughtery's due process rights. (RP 151-52). U.S. Const. amend. XIV; Wash. Const. art. I §22. In allowing this line of questioning, the trial court committed an error of constitutional magnitude. *See Thomas*, 130 Ariz. at 435-36, 636 P.2d at 1217-18; *Estabrook*, 162 Or. at 101, 91 P.2d at 850.

8. Thus, the prosecution used the witness's religious beliefs, which had nothing to do with the issues before the trial court, to make her testimony seem more credible than Mr. Dougherty's testimony. Such use of religious beliefs is prohibited under Const. art I, §11 and ER 610. (Note that *which* is correctly used to introduce a nonrestrictive clause.)

9. Under ER 609(a)(2), when a trial court admits prior conviction evidence of a crime that does not contain an element of deceit, fraud, or false swearing, the trial court commits an error of constitutional magnitude. *State v. Harris,* 102 Wash. 2d 148, 685 P.2d 584 (1984). The rationale for this rule is that while crimes of dishonesty bear directly on a defendant's propensity for truthfulness, other types of crimes do not bear on truthfulness and their admission might serve to prejudice the jury against the defendant.

10. The trial court did not give a cautionary accomplice instruction. This court held that such an instruction is required whenever the prosecution relies solely on accomplice testimony.

✦Exercise 26.J   Pronoun Antecedents

1. The Bloomquists' pre-marital agreement states that Mr. Bloomquist's residuals are community property.

2. Freeman discusses numerous rules of usage in his book, *The Grammatical Lawyer.*

3. From the minutes of the board, we can infer that it knew about the structural weaknesses in the building and decided not to act.

4. Notes made by an attorney during a client interview must be protected under the work-product rule; otherwise, the opposition will have access to the strategy he or she plans to use in the case.

5. The petitioner testified that he did not deliberately shoot anyone.

✦Exercise 26.K Pronoun Review

1. In *Finch*, the petitioner's vehicle collided with the respondent's. The petitioner submitted a claim for property damage to respondent's insurance carrier, which the respondent agreed to pay.

2. Anita Hempstead is a single mother with an 18-month-old daughter. The lights and noise from the night baseball prevent the child from sleeping. This annoyance occurs twice a week. Consequently, Ms. Hempstead claims that the loss of sleep interrupts the child's entire weekly schedule.

3. Upon receipt of Wilson's case, the prosecutor's office treated it in the same fashion as all other referrals. That treatment included processing the police reports, screening them for legal sufficiency, typing and filing an information, and setting an arraignment date with proper notice. Once the prosecutor realized that it could not be routinely processed in the twelve business days between receipt of the police reports and Wilson's eighteenth birthday, he referred the case to the adult division for filing charges.

4. In May of 1986, the president of Glad Tidings Towel Company (GTT) telephoned the president of Smokey Stover Hotels (SSH). The president of GTT said, "I am now responsible for the order." He also told the president of SSH that GTT had completed 20,000 of the 50,000 towels ordered. This information surprised the president of SSH because he had never signed a contract ordering the towels and because it is company policy that the SSH president sign all contracts for orders.

✦Exercise 26.L   Modifier Placement

1. **Just** the deputy prosecutor asked that the plaintiff describe his assailant.

   No one but the deputy prosecutor asked.

   The deputy prosecutor **just** asked that the plaintiff describe his assailant.

   She did not demand or require.

   The deputy prosecutor asked **just** that the plaintiff describe his assailant.

285

She asked for only one thing.

The deputy prosecutor asked that **just** the plaintiff describe his assailant.

Only the plaintiff, no one else should do the describing.

The deputy prosecutor asked that the plaintiff **just** describe his assailant.

Just describe, not draw or point out or name.

The deputy prosecutor asked that the plaintiff describe **just** his assailant.

Just the assailant, no one else should be described.

2. **Only** the defendant claims that the plaintiff was sleeping.

No one else makes this claim.

The defendant **only** claims that the plaintiff was sleeping.

He claims it but cannot prove it.

The defendant claims **only** that the plaintiff was sleeping.

He claims only one thing.

The defendant claims that **only** the plaintiff was sleeping.

No one else was sleeping.

The defendant claims that the plaintiff was **only** sleeping.

Only asleep, not dead

✦EXERCISE 26.M MODIFIER PLACEMENT

1. After Mr. Harper pays alimony and child support, he has **barely** enough money to live on.

2. The court stated that the unavoidable accident defense was appropriate **only** when neither party was at fault and when the party was surprised by sudden changes in circumstances that the party could not reasonably anticipate.

✦EXERCISE 26.N   MISPLACED MODIFIERS

1. The deputy marshal testified that a copy of the complaint was served on the defendant at his Chicago residence on March 12, 1989.

   OR: The deputy marshal testified **that** on March 12, 1989, a copy of the complaint was served on the defendant at his Chicago residence.

2. The duty of a plaintiff in a failed vasectomy is to mitigate damages **only** through a reasonable means; an abortion is not required.

3. The court reasoned that, **given the chance**, many people would be willing to support the unplanned child.

   OR: The court reasoned that many people, given the chance, would be willing to support the unplanned child.

4. Acme Clothing Co. discriminated against Mary Smith when it failed to issue her a new credit card **under her maiden name** for an existing open-ended account.

5. Custom-made towels **imprinted with yellow happy faces trimmed in purple and ordered by the buyer** satisfy the requirement of specially manufactured goods.

6. Harrison Lumber Co., the plaintiff in this action, has filed suit **in federal district court** against our client, Lloyd Putnam, for breach of contract.

7. Hawaii currently does not restrict foreign investment in privately owned real estate; on the contrary, discrimination **based on ancestry** is prohibited in real estate transactions.

8. In *Rovinski v. Rowe*, Robert Rowe brought a personal injury action against Stanley Rovinski for injuries **that he sustained** from an automobile accident.

9. Mrs. Davidson's car collided with Mrs. Howe's car, which was traveling at a lawful rate of speed, **in the middle lane**.

10. The court held that the photographs, **although gruesome,** must be considered in light of the facts needed to be proved by the prosecution.

✦EXERCISE 26.O   DANGLING MODIFIERS

1. In order to answer this question, the court must examine the rule that governs service of process.

2. Applying the majority rule to our facts, the court will find that the benefit of the Bells having a healthy child outweighs the burden.

3. To prove discrimination, Ms. Smith must show that the only difference between her and the others granted credit was Ms. Smith's protected classification.

4. In using the balancing test, the court must consider whether the defendant testified at the prior trial.

5. Comparing *McDonald* to our case, the court will find that the facts are conclusive that Komotios's identification in the police car resulted from impermissibly suggestive police actions.

   OR: Comparing *McDonald* to our case, the court will find that Komotios's identification in the police car resulted from impermissibly suggestive police actions.

7. In measuring monetary damages to real property, courts make two distinctions.

8. In determining what constitutes "appreciable time," the courts have not clearly defined a specific or standard amount of time.

9. Equipment designs are presented to the prospective buyer for approval. Once the design is approved, a bid stating the contract price is submitted.

10. If you wish to collect your pruning fee from Mr. Brown, filing a lien against his orchard may be the best course of action.

1. The defense counsel elicited that the appellant paid for a listed telephone in his own name, kept some clothes and artifacts there, and had a room there that was ready for him to occupy. (The key words, *paid, kept,* and *had*, must match.)

2. As a result of the collision, Rice has suffered a severe concussion, two broken ribs, a lost front tooth, whiplash, and numerous bruises and lacerations. (*Tooth* is now the key word, and it matches *concussion, ribs, whiplash, bruises and lacerations.*)

3. Provisions allowing arbitration are generally upheld because they enhance fair dealing among the parties and prevent litigation. (*Enhance* is parallel with *prevent.*)

4. Chavaria's only reasons for breaking into the locked box in the Senator's desk were his suspicion that it contained the Senator's financial records and his expectation of a probable reward from the Justice Department. OR: Chavaria's only reasons for breaking into the locked box in the Senator's desk were that he suspected that it contained the Senator's financial records and that he expected a probable reward from the Justice Department.

5. The voluminous record in this case contains both substantial and conflicting evidence regarding the sequence of events, the actions of the parties, and the condition of the intersection.

6. The issues for review are whether the trial court abused its discretion by not placing a value on certain items of personal property and by ordering John to pay $600 per month in child support for his four children. (*By not placing* matches *by ordering.*)

7. One factor governing the award of child support includes the cost of caring for, maintaining, and educating the children. OR: One factor governing the award of child support includes the cost of the care, maintenance, and education of the children.

8. The two critical factors in the "instrument or agent" analysis of Fourth Amendment search and seizure law are the government's knowledge and acquiescence in the search and the intent of the party performing the search. (The nouns *knowledge* and *acquiescence* match *intent.*)

9. Clipse described the assailant as wearing a green denim outfit and glasses and having short wavy hair. (The key words *wearing* and *having* are parallel.)

10. To ensure that claimants would be aware of the new act, the Legislature directed the Department of Ecology to publish a statutorily prescribed notice by four different means:

1) **publishing** the notice once a year for five years in major as well as local newspapers; 2) **publishing** the notice every six months on radio and television stations broadcasting in every county; 3) **posting** the notice in a conspicuous location in every county; and 4) **including** a copy of the notice with notices of taxes due for 1972 mailed by each county treasurer.

✦EXERCISE 26.Q   PARALLELISM

1. The trial court concluded that the agreement was not only economically but also procedurally fair.

2. Green fibers that were found to be microscopically indistinguishable from the fibers in Nichol's t-shirt were found both in the car and on the gloves.

3. Mr. Parker claims that the trial court's actions resulted in a property distribution that was neither fair nor equitable.

4. The plaintiff alleges that the City not only failed to erect proper warning signs but also failed to trim obscuring vegetation at the northeast quadrant of the intersection. OR: The plaintiff alleges that the City failed not only to erect proper warning signs but also to trim obscuring vegetation at the northeast quadrant of the intersection.

5. The jury is not to consider this evidence as either proof of negligence or an admission of negligence on the part of the City. OR: The jury is not to consider this evidence either as proof of negligence or as an admission of negligence on the part of the City.

6. The notation on the agent's copy could mean that Peters either made only a quote to Garfield or actually obtained the excess coverage from Munson Insurance.

7. The State can neither take action that will unnecessarily "chill" the assertion of a constitutional right nor draw adverse inferences from the exercise of a constitutional right.

8. In this case, the prosecutor's comments appear to extend more to the defendant's theory of mistaken identity than to his guilt or innocence.

9. The State charged Mookins with one count of assault committed either by using a weapon or instrument likely to produce bodily harm or by knowingly inflicting grievous bodily harm upon the victim.

10. Heller did not object to the use of the medical records evidence either at the board hearing or during the trial de novo in superior court.

Chapter 27
Punctuation

✦**EXERCISE 27.A COMMAS**

1.   . . . by counsel, but he moved . . . .

2.   . . . in the courtroom, and petitioner . . . .

3.   . . . was 21, but he disputed . . . . (No comma after *and* because *and* joins two dependent *that* clauses.)

4.   No comma needed. (The *and* joins two dependent *that* clauses, not two   independent clauses.)

5.   . . . billing practices, yet he expressed . . . .
        (Use of a semicolon before *yet* is also permitted.)

6.   . . . Mafia connections, and one has . . . .

7.   . . . against him, and the record reflects . . . .

8.   . . . was $17,000, and its street . . . . OR
        . . . was $17,000 and its street . . . . (Acceptable to omit comma because clauses are short and closely related.)

9.   . . . minimal, for it was Jones . . . .

10.   . . . false story, but the *Times* . . . .

✦**EXERCISE 27.B COMMAS**

1.   To convict the defendant of the crime charged, the court must find that he had actual knowledge that he was possessing stolen property. (Comma sets off an introductory infinitive phrase.)

2.   In response to DuPont's request, Hommel agreed to accompany DuPont to the rear of the store. (Comma sets off prepositional phrases.)

3. Viewing the evidence in a light most favorable to the prosecution, the trial court found for the defendant. (Comma sets off introductory participial phrase.)

4. In the early morning hours of December 3, 1983, officers from the Houston Police Department were dispatched to an abandoned railroad depot. (Comma sets off two introductory prepositional phrases. Comma would also be required after complete date. See rule 9.)

5. Furthermore, the trial court cautioned the jury to scrutinize separately each defendant's case. (Introductory transitional word must be set off by a comma.)

6. Moreover, to ensure that claimants would be aware of the new act, the legislature directed the Department of Ecology to publish a statutorily prescribed notice.
(First comma sets off transitional expression; second comma sets off introductory infinitive phrase.)

7. When the police conduct a search without a warrant, the state must prove that the particular search or seizure falls within one of the "jealously and carefully guarded" exceptions to the warrant requirement. *Arkansas v. Sanders,* 442 U.S. 753, (1979). (Comma sets off an introductory dependent clause.

8. In *Beck,* the United States Supreme Court held that the death sentence may not constitutionally be imposed for a capital offense when the jury was not permitted to consider any lesser included offenses. (Although the prepositional phrase is short, most legal writers set off case names.)

9. After waiving his right to a speedy trial six times, Martin pleaded guilty to the crime of indecent liberties. (Comma sets off an introductory combination of two prepositional phrases.)

10. However, if the evidence is admissible for one of these purposes, the trial court must determine whether the danger of undue prejudice from its admission outweighs the probative value of the evidence. (First comma sets off a transitional expression; second comma sets off an introductory dependent clause.)

✦EXERCISE 27.C COMMAS

1. Of the twenty, two witnesses are willing to testify.
(Comma needed to prevent reader from seeing *twenty-two* as a unit and assuming that a long introductory phrase was opening the sentence.)

2. During a surveillance, on three successive evenings . . . . (Presumably, the police

observed people exchanging cash for packaged articles on three successive evenings, not that the surveillance occurred on three successive evenings. If the latter is intended, the comma should be placed after *evenings*.)

3. Two years before, the car's brakes failed on a steep mountain road. (Comma needed to prevent reader from initially assuming that this is a long introductory dependent clause.)

4. Once, he had the idea that all women were laughing at him behind his back. (Comma needed to prevent reader from initially assuming that this is a long introductory dependent clause.)

5. Without a doubt, about half the witnesses to the accident will be unwilling to get involved. (Comma needed to prevent reader from assuming that *without a doubt about half the witnesses to the accident* is a long introductory phrase.)

✦Exercise 27.D Commas

1. Trooper Yessler, who investigated the accident, testified that the "primary causal factor" of the accident was Neimeyer's intoxicated state. (Trooper Yessler is completely identified by his name. *Who investigated the accident* adds additional information, not restricting or limiting information.)

2. The state trooper who investigated the accident testified that the "primary causal factor" of the accident had been Neimeyer's intoxicated state. (*Who investigated the accident* is restrictive; it limits the meaning of *state trooper*.)

3. The legislature enacted the Water Rights Registration Act, which required every person who claimed water rights not evidenced by the 1917 or 1945 water codes to register a claim with the State before June 30, 1974. (The name of the act identifies it completely. The nonrestrictive clause adds important additional information, but that information does not restrict or limit the meaning of *Water Rights Registration Act*.)

4. The police talked with a neighbor who had seen a man matching Daniels's description within a block of the Wyatt home on the day of the burglary. (*Who had seen a man . . .* restricts the meaning of *neighbor*.)

5. At about 10:30 p.m., Officer Underwood encountered Norman Rhemn, whom she had observed driving by several times during the evening. (*Whom she observed driving by several times during the evening* adds important additional information to the sentence, but that information does not restrict or limit the meaning of *Norman Rhemn*.)

6. Did the trial court err in giving instruction 9, which sets forth the circumstances

permitting the jury to find whether the petitioner had "actual knowledge" that he possessed stolen property? (*Instruction 9* is completely identified; the *which* clause adds important information to the sentence, but that information does not restrict or limit the meaning of *Instruction 9*.)

7. Those who fail to file waive their water rights. (*Who fail to file* restricts or limits the meaning of *those*, so no commas are needed.)

8. The defendant's conviction was reversed on the ground that the informant was a material witness who could not be subpoenaed by the defense. *Id.* at 1146. (This sentence has two restrictive clauses: 1) *that the informant was a material witness* and 2) *who could not be subpoenaed by the defense*. The first restricts the meaning of *ground*; the second restricts the meaning of *witness.*)

9. The State appealed to Division Two of the Court of Appeals, which reversed and remanded in a published opinion filed August 5, 1986. (The name of the court identifies it completely; the *which* clause adds information that is important to the sentence, but it does not restrict the meaning of *Division Two of the Court of Appeals*.)

10. A polygraph examination is a reasonable extension of those statutory conditions that require a probationer to follow the instructions of his or her probation officer. *See, e.g.*, Wash. Rev. Code 9.95.210. (*Those statutory conditions* is restricted or limited by the *that* clause, so no comma is needed.)

✦EXERCISE 27.E COMMAS

1a. Only those independent contractors who performed the actual dredging are responsible for any negligence.

1b. All independent contractors performed the actual dredging, and all are responsible for any negligence.

2a. Defense counsel will discuss only those factors that favor exclusion of prior conviction evidence.

2b. Defense counsel will discuss all the factors, and all the factors favor exclusion of prior conviction evidence.

3a. There is only one serial number, and it is missing.

3b. There is more than one serial number, but the police are checking only for the one that is missing.

1.   The State has charged the defendant with dealing in a controlled substance, a Class B felony. (Rule 5: *A Class B felony* is a nonrestrictive appositive for dealing in *a controlled substance*.)

2.   . . . motion, arguing that . . . . (Rule 6: Comma sets off nonrestrictive participial phrase.)

3.   The only witness, Ann Peters, had discussed her potential criminal liability with the prosecutor. (Rule 5: *Ann Peters* is a nonrestrictive appositive for *only witness*.)

4.   . . . constitutionally invalid, Lemons . . . . (Rule 6: Comma sets off beginning participle, *contending that his* prior guilty pleas were constitutionally *invalid*.)

5.   (Rule 6: No commas added. *Decision* is modified by the restrictive participial phrase, *affirming his conviction*. If a comma is added after decision, then the sentence means that the Petitioner affirms his own conviction.)

6.   Olson claims that a new trial should have been granted because Nyles, the victim, was available to testify. (Rule 5: *Nyles* is a nonrestrictive appositive for *victim*.)

7.   Correct as is. (Rule 5: *Brennan and Scalia* are not the only Supreme Court Justices, so they are restrictive appositives.)

8.   Campbell's most recent conviction was for second-degree assault, the same crime he is currently charged with committing. (Rule 5: The comma sets off the nonrestrictive appositive.)

9.   Holding that the facts were sufficient to require the submission of the defense of duress to the jury, the Court of Appeals reversed, stating that "[t]he time has come when we can no longer close our eyes to the growing problem of institutional gang rapes in our prison system." (Rule 6: Both participial phrases, *holding that the facts were sufficient to require the submission of the defense of duress to the jury* and *stating that "[t]he time has come when we can no longer close our eyes to the growing problem of institutional gang rapes in our prison system* are nonrestrictive.)

10.   . . .Court of Appeals, assigning error . . . . (Comma sets off nonrestrictive participial phrase and tells reader that Olsen, not Division Two of the Court of Appeals, is assigning error in the appeal.)

✦Exercise 27.G Commas

1. . . . replied, "Sure." (Rule 8: Comma separates introductory words from quotation.)

2. One could infer, therefore, that the billing procedures were there for her to see. (Rule 7: *Therefore* is an interrupter that needs to be set off by commas.)

3. . . . "yes," then . . . . (Rule 8: Commas go inside closing quotation marks.)

4. No commas added. (Rule 8: Quotation is preceded by *that.)*

5. Roberts, however, asserts that she was amenable to process at all times. (Rule 7: *However* is an interrupter that must be set off by commas.)

6. Other cases, on the other hand, suggest that the evidence necessary to satisfy the second prong of the *Workman* test may come from any source. (Rule 7: *On the other hand* is an interrupter that must be set off with commas.)

7. No commas added. (Rule 8: *That* precedes quotation.)

8. Add a comma after *concluded.* (Rule 8: Comma separates introductory words from quotation.)

9. An appellate court may, on its own initiative or by motion of a party, request additional evidence before rendering a decision on a case. (Rule 7: The compound interrupting phrase, *on its own initiative or by motion of a party* is set off with commas.)

10. In *Alford*, the United States Supreme Court held that a plea of guilty is constitutionally valid, in spite of a defendant's claim of innocence, when there was strong evidence of guilt before the trial court and when the plea was a voluntary and an intelligent choice among the alternative courses of action open to a defendant. *North Carolina v. Alford, supra*, at 37-38. (Rule 7: *In spite of a defendant's claim of innocence* interrupts the sentence, so it must be set off with commas.)

✦Exercise 27.H Commas

1. Yesler later identified James in a photo montage, in a lineup, and at trial. (Rule 10: Commas are needed to separate items in a series.)

2. The evidence shows that the defendant was only present at the crime scene, not "ready to assist." (Rule 9: Comma sets off the contrasting phrase.)

3. The prosecutor's comment of disbelief was directed at the defense theory of mistaken identity, not at the credibility of a witness. (Rule 9: Comma sets off contrasting phrase.)

4. Thompson pulled his gun, held it straight up in the air, and told Lew not to bring anyone back. (Rule 10: Commas are needed to separate items in a series.)

5. Thus, the 90-day "time for trial" rule under CrR 3.3(c)(1) began to run when Lewis was arraigned, not when the State filed the information. (Rule 9: Comma sets off contrasting phrase.)

6. The sanity commission concluded that Thomas was incapable of perceiving the nature of his conduct at the time of the offense, was unable to distinguish right from wrong, but was competent to stand trial. (Rule 10: Commas are used to separate items in a series. Also note that the last item in the series is a contrasting element.)

7. The court must follow United States Supreme Court decisions, not a decision by the New Mexico Court of Appeals, when determining whether a defendant is a public or private figure. (Rule 9: Pair of commas set off contrasting phrase.)

8. The *Harris* court held that such an instruction is required whenever the prosecution relies solely on accomplice testimony, but that failure to give the instruction is not reversible error when there is sufficient corroborating testimony. (Rule 9: Comma sets off contrasting element.)

9. Chavez saw a man on the ground, but was unable to identify him because of the darkness. (Rule 9: Comma is used to set off contrasting element.)

10. Jeffreys was arrested for armed robbery, yet was also charged later with second degree burglary. (Rule 9: Comma needed to set off a contrasting element.)

✦EXERCISE 27.1 COMMAS

1. She was taken into custody on May 11, 1987, and arraigned on May 12, 1987. Rule 12: Comma follows the day and year when a full date is used and the sentence continues after the date.)

2. The documents in question mysteriously disappeared from the Dallas office on December 2, 1987, only to reappear in the office in Clovis, New Mexico, on December 9. (Rule 12: Comma follows full date when sentence continues. Comma follows city and state when sentence continues. Sentence is also revised to avoid the awkward *Clovis, New Mexico, office.*)

3. Bennett purchased twelve acres of remote, undeveloped land in central Florida in 1977. (Rule 11: Comma separates coordinate adjectives.)

4. Secret, unexpressed intentions are irrelevant. (Rule 11: Comma separates coordinate adjectives.)

5. Each applicant was required to enclose a self-addressed, stamped envelope with the application form. (Rule 11: Comma separates coordinate adjectives.)

6. Johnston moved to Las Vegas, Nevada, in February .1986 to attend school. (Rule 12: City and state are separated by commas and a comma follows state when sentence continues. No comma between partial date.)

7. The publisher mailed the contract on 1 March 1989 to the author at her address in Cincinnati, Ohio. (Rule 12: No comma when date is in inverted order. The sentence is also revised to avoid the awkward *Cincinnati, Ohio, address*.)

8. "Substantial evidence" exists if it is "sufficient to persuade a fair-minded, rational person of the truth of the declared premise." *See Holland v. Boeing Co.*, 90 Wash. 2d 384, 390-91, 583 P.2d 621 (1978). (Rule 11: Comma separates coordinate adjectives.)

9. Peterson filed his motion to vacate on October 26, 1983, more than two years after the trial court entered the judgment of acquittal. (Rule 12: Comma after full date because sentence continues.)

10. People who received one of these letters were told to "mail $5.00 to the last name and address on the list," which was Amy Andersen, 1813 South Washington, Lawrence, Kansas 66044, or they would suffer "bad luck and other misfortune." (Rule 12: Commas are used to set off individual elements in an address. Comma after zip code when sentence continues.)

✦EXERCISE 27.J COMMAS

1. . . . the blue, another 100 hits. (Rule 14: The comma indicates the omission of "envelope contained.")

2. . . . criminal findings, each based . . . . (Rule 13: *Each based on the same prior convictions* is an absolute.)

3. . . . Jerome's, namely, proceed under . . . . (Rule 15: Some writers may prefer to use a dash before *namely*.)

4.   . . . ; that is, he or she . . . . (Rule 15: Comma sets off expression that introduces explanation.)

5.   . . .--that is, without a valid will-- . . . . (Rule 15: Comma sets off expression that introduces an explanation.)

6.   Melvin Andersen is listed as the president of the corporation; Philip Andersen, the vice-president of operations; Teresa Andersen, the vice-president of internal affairs, and Mary Andersen, the treasurer. (Rule 14: The commas indicate the omission of *is listed as*.)

7.   . . . cut off, Irene . . . . (Rule 13: *Her only source of income cut off* is an absolute.)

8.   . . . valuable possessions, *e.g.*, a three-carat diamond, ... (Rule 15: Comma sets off an expression to introduce an example.)

9.   . . . labelled "successful," Glenda . . . . (Rule 13: *Her surgery having been labelled successful* is an absolute. Also note that the comma goes inside closing quotation marks.)

10.   . . . calls, the first . . . . (Rule 13: *The first less than two hours after the incident* is an absolute.)

✦EXERCISE 27.K UNNECESSARY COMMAS

1.   Omit comma before *if*. (*If* introduces a restrictive adverbial clause.)

2.   Omit comma before *when*. (*When* introduces a restrictive adverbial clause.)

3.   Correct as is. (*Because* introduces a restrictive adverbial clause.)

4.   Omit comma before *as*. (*As* introduces a restrictive adverbial clause.)

5.   No commas needed. (*If* introduces a restrictive adverbial clause.)

6.   . . . practices, although there is no . . . . (*Although* introduces a nonrestrictive clause.)

7.   Omit comma before *unless*. (*Unless* introduces a restrictive adverbial clause.)

8.   Correct as is. (*When* introduces a restrictive adverbial clause.)

9.   Omit comma before *because*. (*Because* introduces a restrictive adverbial clause.)

10. . . . evidence, even though that ruling . . . . (No comma before *when* because it is a restrictive adverbial clause, but a comma is needed before *even though*.)

✦EXERCISE 27.L UNNECESSARY COMMAS

1. The police put a "trap" on the phone, so when the man called the next day, the police were able to trace the call. (Rule 19: Comma is not needed between a conjunction and an introductory clause.)

2. The Hoffelmeirs will probably receive not only the replacement value of the cat but also compensation for their mental anguish. (Rule 18: Do not use a comma to separate correlative pairs.)

3. Defendants may argue that precisely because the plaintiff operates its business in the small community of Lincoln, it holds a position of special prominence in that community sufficient to make it an all purpose public figure. (Rule 20: No comma needed between *that* and an introductory clause.)

4. The fire could reasonably be classified as "manifestly dangerous" because of its intensity, the danger of injury from the propane tanks, and the condition and construction of the barn. (Rule 17: Omit comma separating subject from verb. Revise sentence to avoid the overly long subject.)

5. The *Barr* decision is entitled to much weight in Washington both because it was decided by the full bench of the Washington Supreme Court and because there was no dissenting opinion. (Rule 18: Comma should not separate correlative conjunctions.)

6. Correct as is. (Rule 18: Correlative conjunctions join main clauses.)

7. Wells claims that he was denied his right to cross-examine the representatives of the third-party payors who testified about the payment restrictions. This claim could be valid if he was prevented from negating any inference that he knew the billings were fraudulent. (Rule 17: Do not separate a subject from its verb with a comma. Revise the sentence to avoid an overly long subject.)

8. The court held that when there is a period of delay between filing the information and the arraignment, the time for trial set forth in CrR 3.3(c)(1) begins to run the date the information is filed. (Rule 20: Do not use a comma between *that* and an introductory clause.)

9. The court ruled that although the form was incorrect, the substantive information supplied by the claimant met the legislative intent by "providing adequate records for

administration of the state's waters and notifying the State that the water was being put to beneficial use." *Id.* at 704. (Rule 20: Do not use a comma between *that* and an introductory clause.)

10.   Correct as is. (Correlative conjunctions connect two independent clauses.)

✦EXERCISE 27.M COMMA REVIEW

1.   The Supreme Court held that summary judgment was proper because the State's actions in failing to perform the eye examination and noting an appropriate restriction were totally unrelated to the accident. (No comma before restrictive *because* clause, and no comma for pairs, *failing . . . and noting*.)

2.   At the disposition hearing, the State presented a document describing Nowell's prior criminal history, which consisted of twelve burglary convictions and two minor offenses subject to diversion. (Comma after introductory phrase is correct; another comma must be added before nonrestrictive clause.)

3.   Correct as is. (A comma is needed after the introductory phrase, and commas are needed to set off the nonrestrictive appositive *an escort service.*)

4.   Both contentions will fail if this accident resulted without any warning of Ms. O'Toole's impending blackout. (The comma should be deleted before the restrictive *if* clause.)

5.   Correct as is. (A comma is needed to set off the transition *for example*, and another comma is needed to set off the introductory clause.)

6.   Even though the evidence does not demonstrate that Marvin and Leroy verbalized any plan to carry out the assault, they both appear to have been active participants in the crime. (A comma is needed to set off the introductory clause.)

7.   The first instance of alleged prosecutorial misconduct occurred during closing argument when the prosecutor made several statements concerning Toole's failure to call Doris Simms as an alibi witness. (No comma is needed before the restrictive adverbial clause.)

8.   Owens asserts that the manufacture of a controlled substance may be accomplished only by extraction or chemical synthesis, not by cultivation. (A comma is needed to set off the contrasting element.)

9.   On the evening of February 28, 1977, Atlanta Police Officer Louise Simpson was working undercover on prostitution detail. (Add commas in full date; no comma is needed to set off restrictive appositive.)

10. A waiver to the right to a jury trial must be voluntary, knowing, and intelligent. (To avoid ambiguity, add a comma before the conjunction connecting the last item in a series.)

11. Kevin Morton rode as the "spotter," the person designated to alert the boat driver when the skier falls. (A comma is needed to set off the nonrestrictive appositive, but it should be placed inside the closing quotation marks.)

12. Defense counsel chose to present only one alibi witness, Bertha Owens, who stated that she was in Des Moines, Iowa, at the time of the robbery. (Commas correctly set off the nonrestrictive appositive, but a comma is needed after the state when more sentence follows.)

13. Marie Tao, the defendant's girlfriend, was contacted by an officer who asked if the defendant was there, but she denied knowing anything about his location. (Commas correctly set off the nonrestrictive appositive, but a comma must be added before the coordinating conjunction *but* because it joins two independent clauses.)

14. Mason maintains that, like the convictions in *Mace*, one of his convictions was reversed on appeal and that the habitual criminal finding must likewise be vacated. (Commas correctly set off the interrupter *like the convictions in Mace*, but the comma between the pair of *that* clauses must be deleted.)

15. The Barkers argue that even if the statutory notice is constitutionally adequate, they substantially complied with the requirements of the Water Rights Registration Act. (No comma is needed between *that* and an introductory clause, but a comma is required after the introductory clause.)

16. Correct as is. (No comma is needed before *and* because it connects a pair of dependent clauses.)

17. When Officer Smith asked who had been driving the cars, Pinette approached him and said, "I'm the driver of the Volvo." (A comma is needed to set off the introductory clause, and another comma is needed to set off the explanatory words from the quotation.)

18. This court has warned prosecutors that it will not tolerate the admission of repetitious, inflammatory photographs. (Comma is needed to separate coordinate adjectives.)

19. The Washington State Supreme Court has held that when a case has been appealed and a judgment issued by the appellate court, the trial court may not interfere "by any

proceeding in the cause which is not directed by the appellate order." *State v. Graeber*, 49 Wash. 2d 874, 875, 307 P.2d 563 (1957). (No comma is needed between *that* and an introductory clause, but a comma is needed after the introductory clause.)

20. The appellant placed her daughter in a private, out-of-district school in Denver, Colorado, without first notifying the school district. (A comma is needed to separate the coordinate adjectives, and commas must be added to the geographical name.)

◆EXERCISE 27.N COMMA REVIEW

1. To determine whether the comments
   of a prosecutor denied petitioner a
   fair trial, a court must first determine   rule 2
   if the comments are improper. If they
   are improper, a court must then consider   rule 2
   if there was a "substantial likelihood"
   that the comments affected the jury.
   State v. Reed, 102 Wash. 2d 140, 684 P.2d
   699 (1984). The "substantial likelihood"
   inquiry is premised upon the notion that   rule 20
   although a defendant has a constitutional
   right to a trial by an impartial jury, he   rule 2
   or she is not guaranteed an error-free
   trial. *Id.* at 145; *State v. Davenport*,
   100 Wash. 2d 757, 762, 675 P.2d 1213 (1984).

2. In 1979, the legislature opened a   rule 2
   four-month window during which any claimant
   who missed the prior deadline could
   register a claim. The Barkers, however,   rule 7
   failed to take advantage of this window.
   In 1980, when the Department of Ecology   rule 2
   adjudicated the water rights in the Mohawk
   Creek Basin, the referee concluded that   rule 2
   the Barkers had lost their water rights.
   The Barkers objected to the referee's
   decision, but to no avail, so they then   rule 9
   appealed to Division Three of the Court of   rule 1
   Appeals. The Department of Ecology
   responded by filing a motion on the merits,   rule 4
   which the Commissioner granted in a ruling
   dated July 18, 1985. A motion to modify   rule 12

the Commissioner's ruling was denied on
September 15, 1985.   rule 12

3.   Several days later, two detectives   rule 2
      assigned to the case drove to a woodcutting
      site near Vancouver, Washington, to contact   rule 12
      Hugh Sanders, the man in question. They   rule 5
      found Sanders, identified themselves,   rule 10
      and explained their business. RP. 22-23.
      As they were speaking to Sanders, the   rule 2
      detectives noticed a chainsaw on the ground
      in front of him. Detective Riley, who owned   rule 4
      a Husqvarna chainsaw and was generally
      familiar with that brand, noticed   rule 4
      that the saw had the Husqvarna logo on it,   rule 10
      that it appeared to have been painted red,
      and that its true orange color was showing
      through in several places. RP. 25. When
      questioned, Sanders told the detectives   rule 2
      that the chainsaw was a Homelite, not a   rule 9
      Husqvarna. He added that "they had no   rule 8
      right to touch a man's property."
      Nevertheless, Detective Riley picked   rule 2
      up the chainsaw, examined it, and noticed   rule 10
      that the serial number plate had been
      removed. RP. 25-26. The detectives then
      seized the chainsaw and arrested Sanders,   rule 4
      who was subsequently charged with
      possession of stolen property.

4.   As the Court of Appeals observed, the   rule 2
      trial transcript contains only a brief
      dialogue concerning Bell's representation
      by counsel, and the pretrial hearings,   rule 1,
      which most likely would have addressed   rule 4
      Bell's request for appointed counsel, have   rule 4
      not been transcribed. Thus, the record is   rule 2
      silent on why an attorney was appointed to
      represent Bell and whether Bell validly   rule 10
      waived his right to counsel. Without these
      portions of the record, the Court of   rule 2
      Appeals could not have fully considered
      Bell's claim of self-representation.

5. Petitioner also notes that Division One has apparently applied the *Workman* rule to the facts, not to the statutory elements of the crime. *State v. Gatalski*, 40, Wash. App. 601, 699 P.2d 804 (1985). In *Gatalski*, the Court of Appeals held that even though one can commit attempted kidnapping without also committing the crime of unlawful restraint, the latter crime was, under the facts of that case, necessarily included in the former. *Id.* at 613. The court reasoned that unlawful restraint of another, which is necessary to a conviction for unlawful imprisonment, is a necessary element of first degree kidnapping. Therefore, unlawful imprisonment was properly submitted to the jury as a lesser included offense of attempted kidnapping because actual unlawful restraint was the substantial step taken to complete the crime of attempted kidnapping. In reconciling *Gatalski* with the present case, Division One here noted that attempted kidnapping is a unique crime because it contains the element of "substantial step," which, the court explained, is not and cannot be statutorily defined. Consequently, when unlawful restraint is the substantial step involved in an attempted kidnap, it will "invariably" be an element of the greater offense of attempted kidnapping.	rule 20

rule 9

rule 2
rule 20

rule 2,
rule 7
rule 5

rule 4
rule 4

rule 2

rule 16

rule 2

rule 16
rules 8,4,7
rule 5
rule 2

rule 2 |

✦EXERCISE 27.0 SEMICOLONS

1. license; therefore, (Otherwise the sentence has a comma splice.)

2. act; it OR act. It (The clauses are closely related, so the semicolon is preferable.)

3. permission; therefore, OR Correct as is (The clauses are closely related, so the semicolon is preferable.)

4. license; however, (Otherwise the sentence has a comma splice.)

5. road; Thorndike OR Correct as is (When preceding or subsequent sentence are long, it is better to separate main clauses such as these into separate sentences. If sentence length is not a problem, then the writer may want to use the semicolon to juxtapose the contentions of the opposing parties.)

6. defendant; neither OR defendant. Neither (The semicolon helps to balance one main clause against the other. A period or full stop before the second main clause gives slightly more emphasis to the second main clause.)

7. house; both OR Correct as is (If preceding or subsequent sentences are long, it may be better to separate the main clauses into two sentences. The advantage of connecting both main clauses with a semicolon is that it emphasizes the close relationship between the two main clauses.)

8. observable; he (Otherwise the sentence has a comma splice.)

9. . . . cousins; therefore, (Otherwise the sentence has a comma splice. A colon is also a possible choice. See Section 11.3.)

10. lane; in *Taylor*, OR Correct as is (If preceding or subsequent sentences are long, then it is better to separate main clauses into separate sentences. The advantage of keeping both main clauses in the same sentence is that this structure emphasizes the comparing and contrasting of the two fact situations.)

✦EXERCISE 27.P SEMICOLONS

1. incorrect -- satisfied; the (Otherwise the sentence has a comma splice.)

2. correct -- (Conjunction "but" does not require a semicolon, but one can be used here because the second main clause has internal commas. See p. # in the additional notes on semicolons and their use with coordinating conjunctions.)

3. incorrect -- satisfied; however, (Otherwise the sentence has a comma splice.)

4. correct -- (The first clause is subordinated by "although," so it is not a main clause.)

5. correct -- (The conjunctive adverb "however" occurs in the middle of a main clause, so it is preceded and followed by a comma. The main clauses are correctly separated by a semicolon.)

6.	correct -- (Main clauses are divided by a semicolon, and the two subordinate "if" clauses are separated from their main clauses with commas. See Section 11.1 Rule 2 for punctuation of long introductory clauses.)

7.	incorrect -- search, however, (The first sentence is correctly punctuated, but the second sentence is not. Replace the semicolon after "search" with a comma because the second sentence begins with a clause subordinated by "if"; therefore, it is not a main clause.)

8.	incorrect -- admitted; however, (Otherwise the sentence has a comma splice.)

9.	correct -- (Although this version is correctly punctuated, it forces the writer into an overly long sentence. A better solution is to write two sentences. " . . . search. Therefore, the evidence . . . .")

10.	correct -- (The main clauses are correctly divided and balanced against each other by semicolons.)

✦EXERCISE 27.Q SEMICOLONS

1.	business; the degree . . . another business; and the test of sensibilities, that is, ... (The last item has internal commas.)

2.	warrant; injunctions; damages, which are measured by the loss suffered by the plaintiff; or declaratory judgment. (The third item has internal commas.)

3.	neighborhood; the ratio . . . tenants; and the possible interference with the tenants' comfortable enjoyment of life, with their right to privacy, and with their use of the property as an apartment. (The last item has internal commas.)

4.	Correct (The items are relatively short and do not have internal commas.)

5.	requirements, including the special requirement imposed by the waterfront commission; 2) the fitness . . . restaurant; and 3) the activities . . . . OR Correct as is. (The items are long, and the first item has internal commas. Note that whether the items are numbered in itself does not affect when to use semicolons; however, writers tend to number items when they are long, and long items generally require semicolons.)

6.	winter; offer . . . morning; modify . . . inside; or risk a lawsuit from neighboring businesses. (Some writers may feel that commas are sufficient for separating these items. What is considered a "short" or "long" item varies from writer to writer.)

7.	car; 2) severe . . . median; or 3) swerve . . . . (The items are generally long.)

8. situation; that Linwood has refused to help, despite Hopwood's repeated requests for help; and that . . . . (The second item has internal commas.)

9. intoxicated; 2) the driver . . . vehicle; and 3) the motor vehicle . . . . (Some, if not all, of the items are long.)

10. intoxicated; 2) defendant . . . car; 3) the vehicle . . .   highway; and 4) the keys . . . . (Some, if not all, of the items are long.)

✦EXERCISE 27.R SEMICOLONS

1. exist; consequently (Otherwise the sentence has a comma splice.)

2. the health . . . child; the weight . . . fetus; available
    . . . techniques; and the length . . . determined. (The last item in the series has internal commas, so semicolons are needed to separate the items.)

3. non-viable _ because (No punctuation is required. The second clause, beginning with "because," is a subordinate clause.) For those writers who prefer that the cause come before the effect, the sentence can be revised as follows:

    In *Green*, the court held that viability was a factual issue that must be decided by a jury; consequently, the court refused to rule as a matter of law that a fourteen-week-old fetus was non-viable.

4. Correct as is. (Some writers may choose to use a comma before "but" in this sentence, but both main clauses are relatively long and both contain internal punctuation. Consequently, the semicolon before the coordinating conjunction "but" more clearly separates the two main clauses. See Additional Notes on Semicolons.)

5. discretion; the court OR discretion. The court (Using just a comma after "discretion" produces a comma splice.)

6. reasonable; therefore (Otherwise the sentence has a comma splice.)

7. nuisance; but (Some writers may choose to use a comma rather than a semicolon here, but both main clauses are rather long and both contain internal punctuation. Consequently, the semicolon before the coordinating conjunction "but" separates the two main clauses more clearly. See Additional Notes on Semicolons on p. #.)

8. Correct as is. OR community; public (Use of the semicolon is preferable because the main clauses are not overly long and they are closely related. The semicolon also heightens the comparison.)

9. Correct as is. (Conjunctive adverb "however" is placed in the middle of a main clause, not in between two main clauses.)

10. Correct as is. (Items in the series are long enough to justify using semicolons. Furthermore, each item is itself a main clause.)

✦EXERCISE 27.S SEMICOLONS

1. Correct

2. Correct

3. statute; nevertheless (Change comma to a semicolon to avoid a comma splice.)

4. Correct

5. Correct

6. Correct

7. Correct

8. Correct

9. Correct

10. Correct OR members; so (Some writers prefer to use a semicolon before "so." In this case a semicolon suggests more of a carefully thought out cause-effect relationship; a comma suggests that the second main clause naturally follows out of the first main clause.)

11. Correct

12. car; (Change comma to a semicolon because items in the series are long and contain internal commas.)

13. Correct

14. Correct

15. maintained; and (Change comma to a semicolon because items in series are long and contain internal commas.)

✦EXERCISE 27.T COLON

1. A two-part inquiry is used to determine reliability: 1) was the confrontation procedure suggestive, and 2) under the totality of circumstances, was the identification reliable even if the confrontation procedure was suggestive?

2. Officials who are accorded absolute immunity seem to share one common characteristic: they make discretionary decisions in an adversarial proceeding under time and information constraints.

3. Correct.

4. In California, the service-oriented business persons subject to the bulk sales law are **the following:** the baker, the cafe or restaurant owner, the garage owner, or the cleaner and dyer.

   OR: In California, the service-oriented business persons subject to the bulk sales law are the baker, the cafe or restaurant owner, the garage owner, or the cleaner and dyer.

5.   By requiring independent corroborating evidence only in Miranda situations, the court has adopted what seems to be a radical approach: admissions made in a pre-Miranda setting, at least in DWI cases, do not need corroborating evidence.

6. The defendant is accused of assaulting **the following victims:** Agnes Miller, Denise Donovan, Ellis Emory, and Christine Fremont.

   OR: The defendant is accused of assaulting Agnes Miller, Denise Donovan, Ellis Emory, and Christine Fremont. (No colon needed because the main clause is not a grammatically complete lead-in.)

7.   The court found that the prosecutor's comments during closing argument were not improper **for three reasons:** (1) the witness was "peculiarly available" to the defendant and would have been able to elucidate the events of the crime; (2) the witness has pleaded guilty to a prior crime on the condition that he would not be prosecuted for the crimes charged; and (3) the defendant repeatedly attempted to place responsibility for the charged incident on the witness. *Id.* at 628. (Lead-in main clause is now grammatically complete.)

8.   An investigation revealed that five individuals were at the railroad depot on the night Jones was assaulted: Francis O'Connor, Noel O'Connor, Phillip Whalen, Paul Mendoza, and Tony Rialto. (Do not use a semicolon to set up a list.) 9.RAP 18.8(b) sets forth two criteria for granting extensions of time: (1) there must be "extraordinary circumstances," which refers to the circumstances surrounding the delay, and (2) the extension must prevent a "gross miscarriage of justice," which refers to the merits of the issues to be reaches. *See* L. Orland, *Wash. Practice., Rules Practice* §4523 (3d Ed. 1978).

10.   Correct.

11.   The court in *Petersen* reasoned that a separate covenant is implied between the seller and purchaser "because of the unusual dependent relationship of the vendee to the vendor." *Id.*, 389 N.E.2d at 1158. (No colon because quotation is integrated into writer's sentence.)

12.   For the court to have found for the plaintiffs in *Kelley*, the plaintiffs would have had to establish **the following:**

       (1)the condominium conversion required "extensive rehabilitative construction";

       (2)the defects complained of by the condominium owners were defects of the "new" construction; and

       (3)the defects complained of were "latent" defects. *Kelley*, 478 N.E.2d at 1349.

✦EXERCISE 27.U APOSTROPHE

1.   judge's error. See rule 1.

2.   judges' error. See rule 3.

3.   prosecuting attorney's assistant. See rule 4.

4.   son-in-law's employer. See rule 4.

5.   its. See rule 6.

6.   Terry and Howard's children. See rule 5.

7.   Terry's and Howard's children. See rule 5.

8.   Lois's complaint. See rule 2.

9.   fringe benefits' value. See rules 3 and 4.

10.   two weeks' vacation. See rule 3.

✦EXERCISE 27. V APOSTROPHE

1.   agencies'

2.   Mathewses'

3.   securities'

4.   Davises'

5.   bar examiners'

✦EXERCISE 27.W APOSTROPHE

1.   100's. See rule 8.

2.   prostitutes' clientele. See rule 3.

3.   electricians' union. See rule 3.

4.   franchi*se*' *s*ecurities. See rule 2 on voicing three *s* sounds.

5.   Doris's and Thomas's executors. See rules 2 and 5.

6.   for old times' sake. See rule 2.

7.   change the <u>Mary's</u> to <u>Mari's</u>. See rule 8.

8.   promissory note's validity. See rule 1 and 4.

9.   policies' effects. See rule 3.

10.   tenants' organization. See rule 3.

11.   Schultz's automobile. See rule 1.

12.   Schultzes' automobile. See rule 3.

13. bosses' meeting. See rule 3.

14. the Mayor of New York's statement. See rule 4.

15. Clinton & Nelson's construction company. See rule 5.

16. 1980's. See rule 8.

17. justice of the peace's decision. See rule 4.

18. too many *if*'s. See rule 8.

19. somebody else's problem. See rule 4.

20. whose. See rule 6.

✦EXERCISE 27.X   OTHER MARKS OF PUNCTUATION

1. Correct

2. According to the Bluebook, this quotation is not long enough (34 words) to be single spaced and indented. If the writer is using the Maroon book or a system that allows for shorter block quotations, then the quotation should be indented on the right margin as well.

3. Correct

4. Do not use an ellipsis when the omission occurs at the beginning of a quotation.

5. Do not use an ellipsis before or after a simple phrase that is quoted.

6. Do not use quotation marks around long quotations that are singled spaced and indented.

7. Using the standard enunciated in *Berenson*, the *Kurzius* court held that "[a] zoning ordinance will ***

   OR: Using the standard enunciated in *Berenson*, the *Kurzius* court held the following: "A zoning ordinance will ***

8. Do not use an ellipsis when the omission occurs at the beginning of a quotation.

9. Period goes inside closing quotation marks. "unlawful act."

10.   Do not use quotation marks around long quotations that are singled spaced and indented.

◆EXERCISE 27.Y HYPHENS

1.   Correct
2.   non-stock corporation
3.   Correct
4.   six-month lease
5.   Correct
6.   ex-husband
7.   Correct
8.   all-inclusive report
9.   Correct
10.   fact-finding commission
11.   priest-penitent privilege
12.   low- to moderate-income housing

◆EXERCISE 27.Z HYPHENS

1.   Correct
2.   Correct
3.   Correct
4.   common-law marriage
5.   Chief of Police is correct, but Editor in Chief
6.   cross-examination
7.   Correct
8.   well settled
9.   well-settled
10.   Correct

◆EXERCISE 27.AA COMMA SPLICES AND FUSED SENTENCES

1.   Correct

2.   Comma splice

Corrected:

Mr. Cratchett bought the property sometime in 1988. The facts are in dispute as to the specific month.

3.   Fused sentence

Corrected:

Before Mr. Cratchett bought the property, it was owned by Mrs. Moriarty, who died in October 1987.

4.   Comma splice

Corrected:

Since 1976, the Kearneys have used the property in a variety of ways; for example, they have regularly mowed the grass in the disputed area since 1976 or 1977.

5.   Correct

6.   Correct

7.   Comma splice

Corrected:

When the Kearneys built the patio area, they did not ask Mrs. Moriarty for permission, and Mrs. Moriarty did not object to their use of the area before or after the patio was built.

8.   Correct

9.   Correct

10.   Fused sentence

Corrected:

In September 1988, the Kearneys built a fence between "their" property and Mr. Cratchett's property, and Mr. Cratchett did not object to the fence.

✦Exercise 27.BB Comma Splices and Fused Sentences

Alaska Statute §09.10.030 and the Alaska common law govern the Kearneys claim to quiet title for the disputed strip of land under the doctrine of adverse possession. The court will award the Kearneys title to the land if they can show that their use and possession of the land was continuous for the statutory period, open and notorious, and exclusive and hostile to the record owner.

It is undisputed that the Kearneys have possessed the disputed strip of land for over ten years; however, a problem exists in proving the continuous element because we must also show that the record owner has at no time interrupted the Kearneys' possession of the land. While Mrs. Kearney was alive, she used the land in conjunction with the Kearneys. As a result, this element will have to be decided by a jury.

The second element should be easily satisfied by the Kearneys' improvements to and maintenance of the disputed strip of land. In addition, the Kearneys' use of the land demonstrates that they provided notice to the record holder of their adverse claim.

The Kearneys can satisfy the first half of the third element, exclusive use, by showing that they acted to exclude all other people from the land, although they did allow Mrs. Morarity to use the land while she was alive. Consequently, the first half of this element will have to be decided by a jury.

The Kearneys will argue that they satisfy the second half of the third element, hostile possession. They will show that they acted as any true owner would be maintaining and improving the land. These acts put Mrs. Morarity on notice of the adverse claim, and they show that she acquiesced to the Kearneys' use. These facts will be disputed, however, because Mr. Cratchett will claim that Mrs. Morarity merely gave the Kearneys permission to use her land. As a result, this half of the third element will also have to be decided by a jury.

1. infer

2. principal principal

3. proved

4. When its

5. Either answer is possible, depending on the desired meaning. *Since* means that the treating of the land as your own began at a certain time; *because* means that the making of the improvements caused the treatment of the land as your own.